Table of Contents

How to Use This Workbook

"Freedom of" or "Freedom From" Religion?

Freedom of Speech for the Masses

Freedom to Cover the World Series

Freedom of the Press Under Stress

Permission to "Take it to the Streets"

A Seditious Petition

Examining the Second Amendment

Search Warrants and the Fouth Amendment

Suspending the Right of Due Process: Japanese-American Relocation During WWII

Petitioning the Supreme Court for the Right to an Attorney

Is the Death Penalty a Cruel and Unusual Punishment?

Document Citations

Rights and Reuse

How to Use This Workbook

The Bill of Rights is the first 10 Amendments to the United States Constitution. It spells out Americans' rights in relation to their Government. It guarantees civil rights and liberties to individuals — like freedom of speech, press, and religion. It sets rules for due process of law and reserves all powers not delegated to the Federal Government to the people or the States. And it specifies that just because the Constitution doesn't list every right people have, it doesn't mean those rights not mentioned can be violated.

In this workbook you'll find primary sources to help you explore some of the core concepts, or protections, found in the Bill of Rights, and how they've been tested throughout American history.

Each chapter will lead you to consider the implications of one core concept and includes:

- Background Information
- A key question or questions to frame your thinking
- Questions to help you analyze the document
- A primary source document or documents
- Discussion questions to help you consider the impact or importance of the concept

The concepts covered, in the order they appear in this workbook, include:

- No Law Respecting an Establishment of Religion, or Prohibiting the Free Exercise Thereof (First Amendment)
- Freedom of Speech (First Amendment)
- Freedom of the Press (First Amendment)
- Right of the People Peaceably to Assemble (First Amendment)

- Right to Petition the Government for a Redress of Grievances (First Amendment)
- Right of the People to Keep and Bear Arms (Second Amendment)
- Unreasonable Searches and Seizures (Fourth Amendment)
- Deprived of Life, Liberty, or Property, Without Due Process (Fifth Amendment)
- The Right to Counsel (Sixth Amendment)
- Cruel and Unusual Punishments (Eighth Amendment)

All of the primary source documents included in these chapters come from the holdings of the National Archives. Yet this workbook covers only a small sampling of the protections afforded by the Bill of Rights, and only a few of the billions of primary sources in the holdings of the National Archives.

To explore the Bill of Rights further, visit www.archives.gov/founding-docs/bill-of-rights.

"Freedom of" or "Freedom From" Religion?

For hundreds of years before even the passage of the Bill of Rights, individuals came to our shores seeking the opportunity to worship freely and without persecution. These ideals were solidified in the passage of the First Amendment. It defends an individual's right to worship, but also protects individuals from the government supporting a particular religion: "Congress shall make no law respecting an establishment of religion, or prohibiting the free exercise thereof…"

But what if these two issues come into conflict? How does the First Amendment find balance between the establishment clause and free exercise clause?

Background

In a nationally televised event on Christmas Eve 1968, Apollo 8 astronauts Bill Anders, Jim Lovell, and Frank Borman read the first 10 verses from the book of Genesis in the Bible.

Feeling her First Amendment rights had been violated, American Atheists founder Madalyn Murray O'Hair filed suit against Thomas O. Paine, the administrator of NASA, and the space agency. O'Hair is best known for her role in *Murray* v. *Curlett*, that was consolidated with *Abington School District* v. *Schempp*, and led to the Supreme Court's 1963 ruling that school-sponsored Bible reading in public schools was unconstitutional.

She believed that because the Apollo 8 crew read from the scripture, her rights were infringed upon as an atheist. O'Hair claimed that NASA, a federal agency, instructed the astronauts to read from the Bible and this was a direct violation of separation of church and state. She further alleged that NASA was trying to establish Christianity as the official religion of the United States. As a tax payer, O'Hair argued that federal funds which supported the space program should not be used to accommodate a Bible on board. She also claimed that the date of the Apollo 8 flight was chosen because of religious reasons.

U.S. District Judge Jack Roberts dismissed the suit, writing that the complaint failed to state a cause of action for which relief could be granted. He argued that the plaintiffs were not coerced to watch the televised event, and if the astronauts had been forced to read from the Bible then the personal rights of the astronauts would have been violated, not those of the plaintiffs. Roberts stated carrying the Bible aboard the space capsule neither advanced nor inhibited religion, and therefore did not violate the establishment clause. Roberts concluded that the scheduling of the Apollo 8 flight to coincide with the Christmas season was "approaching the absurd," and "The First Amendment does not require the State to be hostile to religion, but only neutral."

Think About

- What does freedom of religion mean?

- What is the establishment clause? What does it do?

- Does the First Amendment protect someone who is an atheist from being exposed to religion?

Analyze the Document

Consider the following questions as you look at the court opinion on the next pages:

- What claims does O'Hair base her suit on?

- What reasons does Judge Roberts give to dismiss the suit?

Document

The following pages include the opinion that U.S. District Judge Jack Roberts wrote in the *Madalyn Murray O'Hair et al.* v. *Thomas O. Paine, et al.* case.

UNITED STATES DISTRICT COURT
WESTERN DISTRICT OF TEXAS
AUSTIN DIVISION

FILED
DEC 1 1969
DAN W. BENEDICT, Clerk
By _____ Deputy

MADALYN MURRAY O'HAIR, ET AL. []
                                []
VS.   []   CIVIL ACTION NO. A-69-CA-109
                                []
THOMAS O. PAINE, ET AL.   []

MEMORANDUM OPINION

    This is an action brought by Madalyn Murray O'Hair, Richard F. O'Hair and the Society of Separationists, Inc., against Thomas O. Paine, individually and as Administrator of the National Aeronautics and Space Administration [NASA]. The plaintiffs are seeking an order enjoining NASA from (1) doing any act whatsoever which abridges the plaintiffs' freedom from religion or establishes Christianity as the official religion of the United States, and (2) enforcing any policy or regulation which has been heretofore promulgated and which has such above effect. The plaintiffs also seek a temporary restraining order enjoining the defendants "from doing any act whatsoever which restricts or abridges plaintiffs' freedom from religion and specifically enjoining NASA and its administrator and personnel from further directing or permitting religious activities, or ceremonies and especially the reading of the sectarian Christian religion Bible and from prayer recitation in space and in relation to all future space flight activity." Jurisdication of the case is founded upon 28 U.S.C. §1346(a)(2).

    Upon request of the plaintiffs, a three-judge court was convened in accordance with Jackson v. Choate, 404 F.2d 910 (5 Cir., 1968). That Court, consisting of United States Circuit Judge Homer Thornberry, United States District Judge Adrian A. Spears, and United States District Judge Jack Roberts, determined that this case was not properly a three-judge matter. Sardino v. Federal Reserve Bank of New York, 361 F.2d 106 (2 Cir. 1966); Pennsylvania Public Utility Commission v. Pennsylvania Railroad Co., 383 U.S. 281 (1965). The case was accordingly remanded to Judge Roberts for decision.

    The various plaintiffs are atheists, deists, and believers in the complete separation of church and state. They have asserted the right to bring suit in two separate grounds: (1) taxpayer status;

and (2) citizenship status.

In their petition, the plaintiffs have alleged that during the Apollo 8 and Apollo 11 Space Flights, certain astronauts, with the consent or under the orders of NASA, did engage in religious ceremonies in an attempt to establish the Christian religion as the religion of the United States. As a factual basis for such a claim, the plaintiffs have alleged the following: (1) various religious statements were made on television by the astronauts while in space; (2) various items of a religious nature were carried on the spacecraft, thus involving the expenditure of federal funds; (3) certain religious items were depositied on the moon; and (4) the timing of the Apollo 8 flight during the Christmas Season was chosen for religious purposes.

The government has filed a motion to dismiss the plaintiffs' suit for the reason, among others, that the complaint fails to state a cause of action for which relief can be granted. For the reasons set out below, this Court so agrees.

I.

The plaintiffs have alleged that their First Amendment right of freedom of religion has been abridged. This Court has searched the pleadings in vain to find any allegation of coercion. The plaintiffs have neither been forced to do anything nor prohibited from doing anything.

Actually, the plaintiffs have not alleged that their freedom of religion has been abridged but rather that their freedom from religion has been abridged. Apparently, the plaintiffs are claiming that they have a right not to be exposed to religion as they were during the televising of the Apollo 8 flights. This, however, does not amount to coercion, and it is necessary to show a coercive effect to constitute an abridgment of the Free Exercise Clause. Abington School District v. Schempp, 374 U.S. 203, 223 (1962).

The plaintiffs have alleged that the astronauts were ordered to perform these religious activites. There may be an element of coercion here, but it is irrelevant because the plaintiffs must show that their own Free Exercise rights were abridged and not another's. A litigant may assert only his own constitutional rights or immunities. United States v. Raines, 362 U.S. 17, 22 (1959).

II.

In Abington School District v. Schempp, supra, the Supreme Court fashioned a test for distinguishing between forbidden involvements of the state with religion and those contacts which the Establishment Clause permits:

> The test may be stated as follows: what are the purpose and the primary effect of the enactment? If either is the advancement or inhibition of religion then the enactment exceeds the scope of legislative power as circumscribed by the Constitution. That is to say that to withstand the strictures of the Establishment Clause there must be a secular legislative purpose and a primary effect that neither advances nor inhibits religion. P.222

And in Board of Education v. Allen, 392 U.S. 236, Justice Harlan stated in a concurring opinion the following:

> where the contested governmental activity is calculated to achieve nonreligious purposes otherwise within the competence of the State, and where the activity does not involve the State "so significantly and directly in the realm of the sectarian as to give rise to divisive influences and inhibitions of freedom," Abington, at 307, it is not forbidden by the religious clauses of the First Amendment.

Relying upon the above guidelines, this Court must conclude that the government did not abridge the Establishment Clause under the facts as alleged by the plaintiffs.

To begin with, the religious statements of the astronauts while on television were made by the astronauts as individuals and

not as representatives of the United States government. There is
nothing in the pleadings to indicate otherwise. Furthermore, to
have prohibited the astronauts from making these statements would
have been a violation of their own religious rights.

This same reasoning can be applied to the personal religious
items carried by the astronauts of the space flights; this conduct
was clearly protected by their own freedom of religion rights.
To have prohibited the astronauts from taking these items would
surely have violated their own rights, unless of course the space
flight would have been jeopardized.

The plaintiffs have alleged that NASA incurred some
expense in accomodating the astronauts in this matter and that
this was a federal expenditure in furtherance of religion, thus
contravening the Establishment Clause. However, both the
Abington, supra, and the Allen, supra, cases stand for the
proposition governmental activity which benefits religion is
permissible if its primary purpose is secular rather than
religious and if its primary effect neither advances nor inhibits
religion.

The purpose of NASA is obvious: it is solely to accomodate
the astronauts, a perfectly legitimate task especially when one
considers the seriousness of the mission. Literally, a national
effort, consisting of thousands of people, several billion dollars,
and ten years, had been expended to achieve the goals of the space
program. The astronauts were a key factor in the success of this
program, and they were undertaking this mission at great risk to
their own lives. It is approaching the ludicrous to hold that
NASA could not have incurred this minor and incidental expense in
order that the astronauts may attain a greater peace of mind in
this serious undertaking.

The plaintiffs have also alleged that among the items
deposited on the moon were some which had a purely religious
significance and that this violated the Establishment Clause.

However, there are many public ceremonies which have in them some references to God, and these have been held not to be contrary to the Establishment Clause. In Engel v. Vitale, 370 U.S. 421 (1962), Justice Black said the following:

> There is of course nothing in the decision reached here that is inconsistent with the fact that school children and others are officially encouraged to express love for our Country by reciting historical documents such as the Declaration of Independence which contains references to the Deity or by singing officially espoused anthems which include the composers' profession of faith in a Supreme Being, or with the fact that there are many manifestations in our public life of belief in God. Such patriotic or ceremonial occasions bear no true resemblence to the unquestioned religious exercises that the State of New York has sponsored in this instance.

And in Zorach v. Clawson, 343 U.S. 306, 312,3, Justice Douglas said:

> The First Amendment, however, does not say that in every and all aspects there shall be a separation of Church and State. Rather, it studiously defines the manner, the specific ways, in which there shall be no concert or union or dependency one on the other. That is the common sense of the matter. Otherwise the state and religion would be aliens to each other - hostile, suspicious, and even unfriendly. Churches could not be required to pay even property taxes. Municipalities would not be permitted to render police or fire protection to religious groups. Policemen who helped parishioners into their places of worship would violate the Constitution. Prayers in our legislative halls; the appeals to the Almighty in the messages of the Chief Executive; the proclamation making Thanksgiving Day a holiday; "so help me God" in our courtroom oaths - these and all other references to the Almighty that run through our laws, our public rituals, our ceremonies would be flouting the First Amendment. A fastidious atheist or agnostic could even object to the supplication with which the Court opens each session: "God save the United States and this honorable Court."

With regard to the scheduling of the Apollo 8 flight during the Christmas season, it is approaching the absurd to say that this is a violation of the Establishment Clause because of the relgious significance of that date. The First Amendment does not require the State to be hostile to religion, but only neutral.

For all the above stated reasons, it is hereby ORDERED that the motion to dismiss for failure to state a cause of action be, and is hereby, GRANTED.

Signed at Austin, Texas, this 1st day of December, 1969.

JACK ROBERTS
United States District Judge

Discuss

- Do you believe O'Hair's rights were violated? Why or why not?

- Do you agree with the judge's opinion? Why or why not?

Freedom of Speech for The Masses

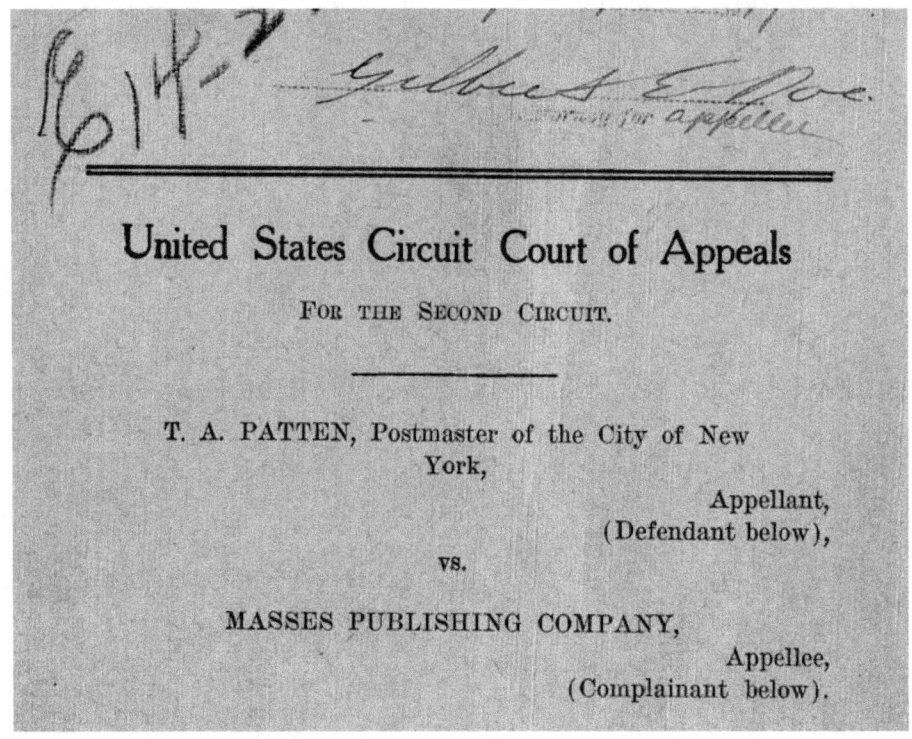

Though freedom of speech is one of our most cherished liberties as protected by the First Amendment, fully enjoying it has not always been possible. This is especially true during times of stress for the nation and government.

Background

During World War I, the Federal Government passed the Espionage Act. Over 2,000 arrests and 1,000 convictions resulted from the passage of the act and its later amendment, commonly called the Sedition Act.

The socialist magazine *The Masses* was dedicated to "radical art and freedom of expression" and "spirited expressions of every kind—in fiction, satire, poetry and essay." For the August 1917 issue, the editors, artists, and writers crafted pieces that showed disapproval for the war.

Draft resisters were praised in an editorial for their "self-reliance and sacrifice." In an introduction to a series of letters from jailed British conscientious objectors, a writer asserted that people could be conscientious objectors without a religious cause. In addition, an article and a poem called anarchists Alexander Berkman and Emma Goldman, recently jailed for speaking out against the draft, "friends of American freedom."

These words were dangerous because of the recent passing of the Espionage Act in June 1917. This law made it illegal to make any statements that would interfere with the military operations, promote the success of the enemy, cause insubordination by soldiers, or obstruct the draft. The maximum sentence was 20 years in jail. The act also gave the Post Office the power to seize any controversial periodical that went through the mail as "non-mailable."

When *The Masses* sent out its August issue, it was seized by New York City's Postmaster T. G. Patten because the "whole tone and tenor" violated the Espionage Act. In the only court case that supported freedom of the press during World War I, Judge Learned Hand agreed with *The Masses* and said that the journal could be mailed. He supported their right to publish by saying nothing within the journal directly advocated resistance to the law.

The Government appealed and eventually indicted seven staff members of *The Masses* for espionage. After two hung juries and with the war already over, the government decided to stop prosecution in the case. Others were not as lucky, and you can see in the cases of Eugene Debs, William Haywood, Mojick Fieron and Anthony Stopa, among others.

Think About

How did the Espionage Act of 1917 limit freedom of speech and freedom of the press?

Analyze the Document

Consider the following questions as you look at selections and cartoons from *The Masses* on the next pages:

- How would you summarize the magazine selections?

- Why does it seem they were written?

- What is depicted in the cartoons? What messages do the cartoons send?

Document

The following pages are Judge Learned Hand's opinion in the court case *The Masses* v. *T. G. Patten*. Look at the last pages (numbered 46-49) to read selections from the journal *The Masses*.

Opinion.

UNITED STATES DISTRICT COURT,

SOUTHERN DISTRICT OF NEW YORK.

MASSES PUBLISHING COMPANY
against
T. G. PATTEN, Postmaster of the City of New York.

The plaintiff applies for a preliminary injunction against the Postmaster of New York to forbid his refusal to accept its magazine in the mails under the following circumstances: The plaintiff is a publishing company in the City of New York engaged in the production of a monthly revolutionary journal called "The Masses," containing both text and cartoons, each issue of which is ready for the mails during the first ten days of the preceding month. In July, 1917, the Postmaster of New York, acting upon the direction of the Postmaster-General, advised the plaintiff that the August number to which he had had access would be denied the mails under the Espionage Act of June 15, 1917. Though professing willingness to excerpt from the number any particular matter which was objectionable in the opinion of the Postmaster General, the plaintiff was unable to learn any specification of objection, and thereupon filed this bill and now applies for a preliminary injunction upon a statement of the facts.

Upon return of the rule to show cause the defendant, while objecting generally that the whole purport of the number was in violation of the law, since

Opinion.

it tended to produce a violation of the law, to encourage the enemies of the United States and to hamper the Government in the conduct of the war, specified four cartoons and four pieces of text as especially falling within sections one and two of Title XII of the Act and by the reference of action one as within section three of Title I. These sections are quoted in the margin.

TITLE I.

Espionage.

Sec. 3. Whoever, when the United States is at war, shall wilfully make or convey false reports or false statements with intent to interfere with the operation or success of the military or naval forces of the United States or to promote the success of its enemies and whoever when the United States is at war, shall wilfully cause or attempt to cause insubordination, disloyalty, mutiny, or refusal of duty, in the military or naval forces of the United States, or shall wilfully obstruct the recruiting or enlistment service of the United States, to the injury of the service or of the United States, shall be punished by a fine of not more than $10,000 or imprisonment for not more than twenty years, or both.

TITLE XII.

Use of Mails.

Section 1. Every letter, writing, circular, postal card, picture, print, engraving, photograph, newspaper, pamphlet, book, or other publication, matter or thing, of any kind, in violation of any of the provisions of this Act is hereby declared to be non-mailable matter and shall not be conveyed in the mails or delivered from any post office or by any letter carrier: *Provided,* that nothing in this Act shall be so construed as to authorize any person other than an employe of the Dead Letter Office, duly authorized thereto, or other person upon a search warrant authorized by law, to open any letter not addressed to himself.

Section 2. Every letter, writing, circular, postal card, picture, print, engraving, photograph, newspaper, pamphlet, book, or other publication, matter or thing, of any kind containing any matter advocating or urging treason, insurrection, or forcible resistance to any law of the United States, is hereby declared to be non-mailable.

The four cartoons are entitled respectively, "Liberty Bell," "Conscription," "Making the World Safe for Capitalism," "Congress and Big Business." The first is a picture of the Liberty Bell broken in fragments. The obvious implication, taking the cartoon in its context with the number as a whole, is that the origin, purposes and conduct of the war have already destroyed the liberties of the country. It is a fair inference that the Draft Law is an especial instance of the violation of the liberty and fundamental rights of any free people.

The second cartoon shows a cannon to the mouth of which is bound the naked figure of a youth to the wheel, that of a woman, marked "Democracy," and upon the carriage that of a man, marked "Labor." On the ground kneels a draped woman marked "Motherhood" in a posture of desperation, while her infant lies on the ground, the import of this cartoon is obviously that conscription is the destruction of youth, democracy and labor, and the desolation of the family. No one can dispute that it was intended to rouse detestation for the Draft Law.

The third cartoon represents a Russian workman symbolizing the Workmen's and Soldiers' Council, seated at a table, studying a paper entitled "Plan for a Genuine Democracy." At one side Senator Root furtively approaches the figure with a noose marked "Advice," apparently prepared to throw it over the head of the workman, while behind him stands Mr. Charles E. Russell, the Socialist member of the Russian Commission, in a posture of assent. On the other side a minatory figure of Japan appears through a door carrying a raised sword marked "Threat," while behind him follows a conventional John Bull, stirring him up to action. The import again is unambiguous and undisputed. The Russian is being ensnared and bullied by the United States and its Allies into continuance of the war for purposes prejudicial to true democracy.

The fourth and last cartoon presents a collection of pursy magnates standing about a table on which lies a map, entitled "War Plans." At the door enters an apologetic person, hat in hand, diffidently standing at the threshold, while one of the magnates warns him to keep off. The legend at the bottom runs as follows: "Congress: 'Excuse me, gentlemen—where do I come in?' Big Business: 'Run along now—we got through with you when you declared war for us.'" It is not necessary to expatiate upon the import of this cartoon.

The four pieces of text are annexed to the end of this report as addenda, A., B., C. and D. After that part of B., so set forth, the article continues, showing the hardships and maltreatment of a number of English conscientious objectors, partly from excerpts out of their letters, partly from reports of what they endured. These statements show much brutality in the treatment of these persons.

The challenged text, omitting the excerpts just mentioned, total about one page out of a total of twenty-eight. Throughout the rest are sprinkled other text designed to arouse animosity to the draft and to the war, and criticisms of the President's consistency in favoring the declaration of war.

The defendant attaches to its papers as well copies of the June and July numbers of "The Masses" and a number of "Mother Earth," a magazine edited by Emma Goldman and Alexander Berkman, recently convicted in this Court for a conspiracy to resist the draft. The earlier copies of "The Masses" contain inflammatory articles upon the war and conscription in revolutionary vein, some of which go to the extent of counselling those subject to conscription to resist. This case does not concern them except in so far as the defendant's position is correct that in the interpretation of the August number the purpose of the writers may be inferred from what preceded and that an audience addressed in the earlier numbers would put upon the later number a significance beyond what the contents would naturally bear if it stood alone. It is not necessary for a determination of this case to set forth in detail the contents of these numbers. The copy of "Mother Earth" also need not be referred to.

GILBERT E. ROE, for the Plaintiff.

EARL B. BARNES, Assistant United States Attorney, for the Defendant.

LEARNED HAND, D. J.: It is well settled that this Court has jurisdiction to review the act of the Postmaster, School of Magnetic Healing vs. McAnnulty, 187 U. S., 94; Post Publishing Co. vs. Murray, 230 Fed. R., 773; Bruce vs. United States, 202 Fed. R., 98; United States vs. Atlanta Journal, 210 Fed. R., 275. If it appears that his proposed official course is outside of the authority conferred upon him by law, this Court cannot escape the duty of so deciding, just as in the case of any other administrative officer, Noble vs. Union River Logging Co., 147 U. S., 165; Gegiow vs. Uhl, 239 U. S., 3. However, again, as in the case of other such officers, the Postmaster's decision is final if there be any dispute of fact upon which his decision may rest, and even where it must turn upon a point of law, it has a strong presumption of validity. Bates & Guild Co. vs. Payne, 194 U. S., 106; Public Clearing House vs. Coyne, 194 U. S., 497. In this case there is no dispute of fact which the plaintiff can successfully challenge except the meaning of the words and pictures in the magazine. As to these the query must be, what is the extreme latitude of the interpretation which must be placed upon them, and whether that extremity certainly falls outside any of the provisions of the Act of June 15, 1917. Unless this be true the decision of the Postmaster must stand. It will be necessary, first to interpret the law and next the words and pictures.

It must be remembered at the outset—and the distinction is of critical consequence throughout—that no question arises touching the war powers of Congress. It may be that Congress may forbid the mails to any matter which tends to discourage the successful prosecution of the war. It may be that the fundamental personal rights of the individual must stand in abeyance even including the right of the freedom of the press, though that is not here in question. Ex parte Jackson, 96 U. S., 727; Re Rapier, 143 U. S., 110. It may be that the peril of war which goes to the very existence of the State justifies any measure of compulsion, any measure of suppression, which Congress deems necessary to its safety, the liberties of each being in subjection to the liberties of all. The Legal Tender Cases, 12 Wall., 457. It may be that under the war power, Congress may mobilize every resource of men and materials, without impediment or limitation, since the power includes all means which are the practice of nations in war. It would indeed not be necessary, perhaps in ordinary cases it would not be appropriate, even to allude to such putative incidents of the war power, but it is of great consequence at the present time with accuracy to define the exact scope of the question at bar, that no implication may arise as to any limitation upon the absolute and uncontrolled nature of that power. Here is presented solely the question of how far Congress after much discussion has up to the present time seen fit to exercise a power which may extend to measures not yet even considered, but necessary to the existence of the State as such. No one suggests that the exercise of such power, however wide it may be, does not rest in Congress alone, at least subject to martial law which may rest with the President within the sphere of military operations, however broadly that may be defined. The defendant's authority is based upon the Act of Congress and the intention of that act is the single measure of that authority. If Congress has omitted repressive measures necessary to the safety of the nation and success of its great enterprise, the responsibility rests upon Congress and with it the power to remedy that omission.

Coming to the act itself it is conceded that the defendant's only direct authority arises from Title XII of the Act, sections one and two. His position is that under section one any writing which by its utterance would infringe any of the provisions of other titles in the Act becomes non-mailable. I may accept that assumption for the sake of argument and turn directly to section three of Title I, which the plaintiff is said to violate. That section contains three provisions. The first is in substance that no one shall make any false statements with intent to interfere with the operation or success of the military or naval forces of the United States or to promote the success of its enemies. The defendant says that the cartoons and text of the magazine constituting as they certainly do, a virulent attack upon the war and those laws which have been enacted to assist its prosecution, may interfere with the success of the military forces of the United States. That such utterances may have the effect so ascribed to them is unhappily true; publications of this kind enervate public feeling at home which is their chief purpose, and encourage the success of the enemies of the United States abroad, to which they are generally indifferent. Dissension within a country is a high source of comfort and assistance to its enemies; the least intimation of it they seize upon with jubilation. There cannot be the slightest question of the mischievous effects of such agitation upon the success of the national project, or of the correctness of the defendant's position.

All this, however, is beside the question whether such an attack is a wilfully false statement. That phrase properly includes only a statement of fact which the utterer knows to be false, and it cannot be maintained that any of these statements are of fact, or that the plaintiff believes them to be false. They are all within the range of opinion and of criticism; they are all certainly believed to be true by the utterer. As such they fall within the scope of that right to criticise either by temperate reasoning, or by immoderate and indecent invective which is normally the privilege of the individual in countries dependent upon the free expression of opinion as the ultimate source of authority. The argument may be trivial in substance, and violent and perverse in manner, but so long as it is confined to abuse of existing policies or laws, it is impossible to class it as a false statement of facts of the kind here in question. To modify this provision, so clearly intended to prevent the spreading of false rumors which may embarrass the military, into the prohibition of any kind of propaganda, honest or vicious, is to disregard the meaning of the language, established by legal construction and common use, and to raise it into a means of suppressing intemperate and inflammatory public discussion, which was surely not its purpose.

The next phrase relied upon is that which forbids anyone from wilfully causing insubordination, disloyalty, mutiny or refusal of duty in the military or naval forces of the United States. The defendant's position is that to arouse discontent and disaffection among the people with the prosecution of the war and with the draft tends to promote a mutinous and insubordinate temper among the troops. This, too, is true; men who become satisfied that they are engaged in an enterprise dictated by the unconscionable selfishness of the rich, and effectuated by a tyrannous disregard for the will of those who must suffer and die, will be more prone to insubordination than those who have faith in the cause and acquiesce in the means. Yet to interpret the word "cause" so broadly would, as before, involve necessarily as a consequence the suppression of all hostile criticism, and of all opinion except what encouraged and supported the existing policies, or which fell within the range of temperate argument. It would contradict the normal assumption of democratic government that the suppression of hostile criticism does not turn upon the justice of its substance or the decency and propriety of its temper. Assuming that the power to repress such opinion may rest in Congress in the throes of a struggle for the very existence of the State, its exercise is so contrary to the use and want of our people, that only the clearest expression of such a power justifies the conclusion that it was intended.

The defendant's position, therefore, in so far as it involves the suppression of the free utterance of abuse and criticism of the existing law, or of the policies of the war, is not, in my judgment, supported by the language of the Statute. Yet there has always been a recognized limit to such expressions, incident indeed to the existence of any compulsive power of the State itself. One may not counsel or advise others to violate the law as it stands. Words are not only the keys of persuasion, but the triggers of action, and those which have no purport but to counsel the violation of law cannot by any latitude of interpretation be a part of that public opinion which is the final source of government in a democratic state. The defendant asserts not only that the magazine indirectly through its propaganda leads to a disintegration of loyalty and a disobedience of law, but that in addition it counsels and advises resistance to existing law, especially to the draft. The consideration of this aspect of the case more properly arises under the third phrase of section three, which forbids any wilful obstruction of the recruiting or enlistment service of the United States, but as the defendant is to urge that the magazine falls within each phrase it is as well to take it up now. To counsel or advise a man to an act urges upon him either that it is his interest or his duty to do it. While, of course, this may be accomplished as well by indirection as expressly, since words carry the meaning that they import, the definition is exhaustive, I think, and I shall use it. Political agitation, by the passions it arouses or the convictions it engenders, may in fact stimulate men to to the violation of law. Detestation of existing policies is easily transformed into forcible resistance of the authority which puts them in execution, and it would be folly to disregard the causal relation between the two. Yet to assimilate agitation, legitimate as such, with direct incitement to violate resistance is to disregard the tolerance of all methods of political agitation which in normal times is a safeguard of free government. The distinction is not a scholastic subterfuge, but a hard-bought acquisition in the fight for freedom, and the purpose to disregard it must be evident when the power exists. If one stops short of urging upon others that it is their duty or their interest to resist the law, it seems to me one should not be held to have attempted to cause its violation. If that be not the test, I can see no escape from the conclusion that under this section every political agitation which can be shown to be apt to create a seditious temper is illegal. I am confident that by such language Congress had no such revolutionary purpose in view.

It seems to me, moreover, quite plain that none of the language and none of the cartoons in this paper can be thought directly to counsel or advise insubordination or mutiny, without a violation of their meaning quite beyond any tolerable understanding. I come, therefore, to the third phrase of the section which forbids anyone from wilfully obstructing the recruiting or enlistment service of the United States. I am not prepared to assent to the plaintiff's position that this only refers to acts other than words, nor that the act thus defined must be shown to have been successful. One may obstruct without preventing and the mere obstruction is an injury to the service, for it throws impediments in its way. Here again, however, since the question is the expression of opinion I construe the sentence, so far as it restrains public utterance, as I have construed the other two, and as therefore limited to the direct advocacy of resistance to the recruiting and enlistment service. If so, the inquiry is narrowed to the question whether any of the challenged matter may be said to advocate resistance to the draft, taking the meaning of the words with the utmost latitude which they can bear.

As to the cartoons it seems to me quite clear that they do not fall within such a test. Certainly the nearest is that entitled "Conscription" and the most that can be said of that is that it may breed such animosity to the draft as will promote resistance and strengthen the determination of those disposed to be recalcitrant. There is no intimation that, however, hateful the draft may be one is in duty bound to resist it, certainly none that such resistance is to one's interest. I cannot, therefore, even with the limitations which surround the power of the Court, assent to the assertion that any of the cartoons violate the act.

The text offers more embarrassment. The poem to Emma Goldman and Alexander Berkman, at most goes no further than to say that they are martyrs in the cause of love among nations. Such a sentiment holds them up to admiration and hence their conduct to possible emulation. The paragraph in which the editor offers to receive funds for their appeal also expresses admiration for them, but goes no further. The paragraphs upon conscientious objectors are of the same kind. They go no further than to express high admiration for those who have held and are holding out for their convictions even to the extent of resisting the law. It is plain enough that the paper has the fullest sympathy for these people; that it admires their courage and that it presumptively approves their conduct. Indeed, in the earlier numbers and before the draft went into effect the editor urged resistance. Since I must interpret the language in the most hostile sense, it is fair to suppose, therefore, that these passages go as far as to say: "These men and women are heroes and worthy of a freeman's admiration. We approve their conduct; we will help to secure them their legal rights. They are working for the betterment of mankind through their obdurate consciences." Moreover, these passages it must be remembered occur in a magazine which attacks with the utmost violence the draft and the war. That such comments have a tendency to arouse emulation in others is clear enough, but that they counsel others to follow these examples is not so plain. Literally at least they do not, and while, as I have said, the words are to be taken not literally, but according to their full import, the literal meaning is the starting point for interpretation. One may admire and approve the course of a hero without feeling any duty to follow him. There is not the least implied intimation in these words that others are under a duty to follow. The most that can be said is that if others do follow they will get the same admiration and the same approval. Now there is surely an appreciable distance between esteem and emulation; and unless there is here some advocacy of such emulation I cannot see how the passages can be said to fall within the law. If they do, it would follow that while one might express admiration and approval for the Quakers or any established sect which is excused from the draft, one could not legally express the same admiration and approval for others who entertain the same conviction, but do not happen to belong to the Society of Friends. It cannot be that the law means to curtail such expressions merely, because the convictions of the class within the draft are stronger than their sense of obedience to the law. There is ample evidence in history that the Quaker is as recalcitrant to legal compulsion as any man; his obstinacy has been regarded in the act, but his disposition is as disobedient as that of any other conscientious objector. Surely, if the draft had not excepted Quakers, it would be too strong a doctrine to say that any who openly admired their fortitude or even approved their conduct was wilfully obstructing the draft.

When the question is of a statute constituting a crime it seems to me that there should be more definite evidence of the act. The question before me is similar to what would arise upon a motion to dismiss an indictment at the close of the proof; could any reasonable man say, not that the indirect result of the language might be to arouse a seditious disposition, for that would not be enough, but that the language directly advocated resistance to the draft? I cannot think that upon such language any verdict would stand. Of course the language of the statute cannot have one meaning in an indictment and another when the case comes up here, because by hypothesis if this paper is non-mailable under section three of Title I, its editors have committed a crime in uttering it.

After the foregoing discussion it is hardly necessary to speak of section two of Title XII. The plaintiff insists that refusal to comply with the provisions of the draft cannot be classed as forcible resistance; that such a refusal is at most only inaction, the neglect of an affirmative duty even to the extent of submitting to imprisonment. It may be plausibly contended that by forcible resistance Congress meant more than passive resistance; but even if this be not true, the result is the same, because so construed the section goes no further than the last phrase of section three of Title I as I have construed it here. What was, therefore, said upon that section will serve here.

The defendant's action was based, as I understand it, not so much upon the narrow question whether these four passages actually advocated resistance, though that point was distinctly raised, as upon the doctrine that the general tenor and animus of the paper as a whole were subversive to authority and seditious in effect. I cannot accept this test under the law as it stands at present; the addition of English-speaking freedom has depended in no small part upon the merely procedural requirement that the State point with exactness to just that conduct which violates the law. It is difficult and often impossible to meet the charge that one's general ethos is treasonable; such a latitude for construction implies a personal latitude in administration which contradicts the normal assumption that law shall be embodied in general propositions capable of some measure of definition. The whole crux of this case turns indeed upon this thesis. I make no question of the power of Congress to establish a personal censorship of the press under the war power; that question, as I have already said, does not arise. I am quite satisfied that it has not yet chosen to create one, and with the greatest deference it does not seem to me that anything here challenged can be illegal upon any other assumption.

Finally, the question arises as to how far the earlier numbers of the paper should be considered. The theory is that the August number covertly refers to the explicit counsel of resistance in the numbers of June and July. A priori such a reference might legitimately incorporate the earlier expressions; I do not doubt that the memory of those expressions may in fact remain in the minds of readers, and that they may be revived by the sympathy and accord with conscientious objectors, expressed in the August number. Yet the plaintiff is still entitled to ask, whatever the results of its past utterance may be, that some words be pointed out which by some reference fairly inferable from the words themselves relate back to earlier and more explicit statements. I think there are no words in the four passages which admit of such an interpretation.

It follows that the plaintiff is entitled to the usual preliminary injunction.

July 24th, 1917.

L. H.,
D. J.

"A."

A Question.

Often I wish we had a continuing census bureau to which we might apply, and have a census taken with classifications of our own choosing. I would like to know to-day, how many men and women there are in America who admire the self-reliance and sacrifice of those who are resisting the conscription law on the ground that they believe it violates the sacred rights and liberties of man. How many of the American population are in accord with the American press when it speaks of the arrest of these men of genuine courage as a "Round-up of Slackers"? Are there none to whom this picture of the American republic adopting toward its citizens the attitude of a rider toward cattle is appalling? I recall the Essays of Emerson, the Poems of Walt Whitman, which sounded a call never heard before in the world's literature, for erect and insuppressible individuality, the courage of solitary faith and heroic assertion of self. It was America's contribution to the ideals of man. It painted the quality of her culture for those in the old world who loved her. It was a revolt of the aspiring mind against that instinctive running with custom and the support of numbers, which is an hereditary frailty of our nerves. It was a determination to worship and to love, in the living and laughing present, the same heroisms that we love when we look back so seriously over the past.

I wonder if the number is few to whom this high resolve was the distinction of our American idealism, and who feel inclined to bow their heads to those who are going to jail under the whip of the State, because they will not do what they do not believe in doing. Perhaps there are enough of us, if we make ourselves heard in voice and letter, to modify this ritual of contempt in the daily press, and induce the American government to undertake the imprisonment of heroic young men with a certain sorrowful dignity that will be new in the world.

"B."

A Tribute.

Emma Goldman and Alexander Berkman
    Are in prison,
Although the night is tremblingly beautiful
And the sound of water climbs down the rocks
And the breath of the night air moves through
    multitudes and multitudes of leaves
That love to waste themselves for the sake of the
    summer.

Emma Goldman and Alexander Berkman
Are in prison tonight,
But they have made themselves elemental forces,
Like the water that climbs down the rocks:
Like the wind in the leaves:
Like the gentle night that holds us:
They are working on our destinies:
They are forging the love of the nations:
*   *   *   *   *   *   *

Tonight they lie in prison.

"C."
Conscientious Objectors.

We publish below a number of letters written last year from English prisons by conscientious objectors. It is as yet uncertain what treatment the United States government will mete out to its thousands of conscientious objectors, but we believe that our protestors against government tyranny will be as steadfast as their English comrades. It is not by any means as certain that they will be as polite to their guards and tormentors, but we hope they will remember that these are acting under official compulsion and not as free men.

Some discussion has arisen as to whether those whose objection to participating in war is not embodied in a religious formula, have the right to call their objection a "conscientious" one. We believe that this old-fashioned term is, however, one that fits their case. There are some laws which the individual feels that he *cannot obey*, and which he will suffer any punishment, even that of death, rather than recognize as having authority over him. This fundamental stubbornness of the free soul against which all the powers of the state are helpless, constitutes a conscientious objection, whatever its original sources may be in political or social opinion. It remains to be demonstrated that a political disapproval of *this* war can express itself in the same heroic firmness that has in England upheld the Christian objectors to war-as-murder. We recommend to all who intend to stick it out to the end, a thorough reading of the cases which follow, so that they may be prepared for what is at least rather likely to happen to them.

"D."

Friends of American Freedom.

Alexander Berkman and Emma Goldman have been arrested, charged with advocating in their paper, *Mother Earth*, that those liable to the military draft, who do not believe in the war, should refuse to register. That they would be arrested, on some charge, and subjected to bitter prosecution, has been inevitable ever since they appeared as the spokesmen of a working-class protest against the plans of American militarism. Whatever you may think of the practicability of such a protest, you must, with their friends, pay tribute of admiration for their courage and devotion.

Alexander Berkman is one of the few men whose character and intelligence ever stood firm through a quarter of a lifetime in prison. Emma Goldman has followed her extreme ideal of liberty for thirty years, up and down, in better places and worse than the federal pentitentiary. They can both endure what befalls them. They have more resources in their souls, perhaps, as they have the support of a more absolute faith, than we have who admire them. But let us give them every chance for acquittal that the constitution of the times allow. Let us give them every chance to state their faith. The Masses will receive funds for this purpose.

Document

Explore the political cartoons from *The Masses* that were cited in the opinion. Go to the website of the Tamiment Library and Robert Wagner Labor Archives at New York University at http://dlib.nyu.edu/themasses/books/masses076 and navigate to pages 4, 7, 26-27, and 33.

Discuss

Look at page 3 of the Espionage Act at https://www.docsteach.org/documents/document/espionage-act and read sections 3 and 4 to help you think about the following:

- Did the *The Masses* violate the Espionage Act? If yes, which selections were in violation?

- Does the government have the right to restrict freedom of the press during wartime? Why or why not?

- Do you think the Espionage Act of 1917 was constitutional? Why or why not?

Freedom to Cover the World Series

Baseball and social change have been linked since Jackie Robinson broke the color line in 1947. *Sports Illustrated* reporter Melissa Ludtke broke another line 30 years later when she sued Commissioner of Baseball Bowie Kuhn to gain access to the locker room. This "gender line" in the reporting of sports calls out First Amendment-guaranteed freedom of the press (and the 14th Amendment's equal protection clause).

Background

After rising through the ranks as a junior reporter, Melissa Ludtke was assigned to cover the 1977 baseball playoffs and World Series. During the first two American League playoff games in New York, the Yankees refused to provide her the same access to the locker room as her male colleagues.

Before the World Series started, Los Angeles Dodger players voted to let Ludtke into the clubhouse after games. But Baseball Commissioner Bowie Kuhn stepped in and reversed this decision. Ludtke missed capturing the ballplayers' locker-room stories and interviews.

Game 6 had included perhaps one of the best individual performances in baseball history. During that game, Yankees star Reggie Jackson earned the nickname "Mr. October" by hitting three straight home runs on three straight pitches (from three different pitchers, no less). The Yankees would win their first World Series in over a decade; but Ludtke would not be allowed to interview Reggie or others about it in the locker room.

When the 1978 baseball season approached, Ludtke and Time, Inc. (the parent company of *Sports Illustrated*) filed suit against Bowie Kuhn, the New York Yankees, Mayor of New York City Abraham Beame, and other officials. In the complaint, they alleged discrimination on 14th Amendment grounds since she was being deprived of the "opportunity to cover baseball in the same manner and to the same extent as her male colleagues and competitors." Her First Amendment rights were infringed, they alleged, when she was denied "fair access to a source of news."

In the judgment, the court ordered the New York Yankees to allow Melissa Ludtke and all female accredited sports reporters access to the clubhouse locker rooms. Ludtke's case opened baseball locker-room doors to female reporters, growing at that time to about 50% of journalists.

Think About

- Should there ever be limits on freedom of the press, as guaranteed by the First Amendment?

- If yes, what might those limits be?

Analyze the Document

Consider the following questions as you look at the court case complaint on the next pages:

- Who and what are involved?

- What specific arguments and reasoning did Ludtke and her lawyers use?

- What did Ludtke and her lawyers ask for?

Document

The following pages show pages 13-16 of a complaint from the court case in which *Sports Illustrated* journalist Melissa Ludtke alleged that Major League Baseball's policy of excluding female reporters from locker rooms put her at a professional disadvantage because of her gender.

was unlawful, and asking them to change the policy for the forthcoming season. Each of those defendants has declined or failed to agree to change the policy.

39. The City has failed to take any steps to avoid or redress the policy of excluding accredited female reporters from the clubhouse, under the provisions of the lease empowering the City to assure compliance by the New York Yankees with their duty to comply with federal, state and local laws.

Count I

40. Plaintiffs repeat each and every allegation contained in paragraphs 1 through 39.

41. By reason of the foregoing, plaintiff Ludtke was deprived and is being deprived of the opportunity to cover baseball in the same manner and to the same extent as her male colleagues and competitors.

42. By reason of the foregoing, plaintiff Time was deprived and is being deprived of the right to make the best use of its reporters based on their talent and expertise and thus of the opportunity to give the coverage it wishes to give to baseball.

43. Defendants' conduct constitutes an unlawful discrimination on the basis of sex and violates 42 U.S.C. § 1983 in that it deprives plaintiffs of the

equal protection of the laws secured and guaranteed by
the Fourteenth Amendment to the United States Constitution.

Count II

44. Plaintiffs repeat each and every allegation contained in paragraphs 1 through 39, 41 and 42.

45. Defendants' conduct denies plaintiffs fair access to a source of news to which the press generally has been granted access and violates 42 U.S.C. § 1983 in that it deprives plaintiffs of the freedom of the press secured and guaranteed by the First Amendment to the United States Constitution as applied to the States through the Fourteenth Amendment to the United States Constitution.

Count III

46. Plaintiffs repeat each and every allegation contained in paragraphs 1 through 39, 41 and 42.

47. Defendants' conduct constitutes an unlawful discrimination on the basis of sex and is an unlawful discriminatory practice under Section 296(2) of the New York Executive Law.

Count IV

48. Plaintiffs repeat each and every allegation contained in paragraphs 1 through 39, 41 and 42.

49. Defendants' conduct constitutes an unlawful discrimination on the basis of sex and deprives plaintiffs of the equal protection of the laws secured and guaranteed by Article I, Section 11 of the New York State Constitution.

Count V

50. Plaintiffs repeat each and every allegation contained in paragraphs 1 through 39, 41 and 42.

51. Defendants' conduct denies plaintiffs fair access to a source of news to which the press generally has been granted access and deprives plaintiffs of the freedom of the press secured and guaranteed by Article I, Section 8 of the New York State Constitution.

WHEREFORE Plaintiffs pray judgment against defendants as follows:

(a) such damages as shall be proved;

(b) an injunction enjoining defendants and anyone subject to their direction and control from denying plaintiff Ludtke and any other accredited representatives of plaintiff Time access to professional baseball clubhouses on the ground of their sex;

(c) an injunction requiring the City to proceed under its lease to secure compliance by the New York Yankees with federal, state and local laws prohibiting discrimination;

 (d) an award of reasonable attorneys' fees; and

 (e) such other and further relief as this Court may deem just and proper.

      CRAVATH, SWAINE & MOORE,

      by *Frederick A. O. Schwarz, Jr.*
        A Member of the Firm

      Attorneys for Plaintiffs,
      One Chase Manhattan Plaza,
      New York, N. Y. 10005.

Discuss

- Imagine the response provided by Major League Baseball. What arguments would they make to deny entry to the locker room? Are any of those arguments valid?

- Read the Order and Judgment at https://www.docsteach.org/documents/document/order-with-notice-of-entry-judgment. How big of an impact do you think this decision had on sports media?

- How do you think sports reporting would be different today without this decision?

Freedom of the Press Under Stress

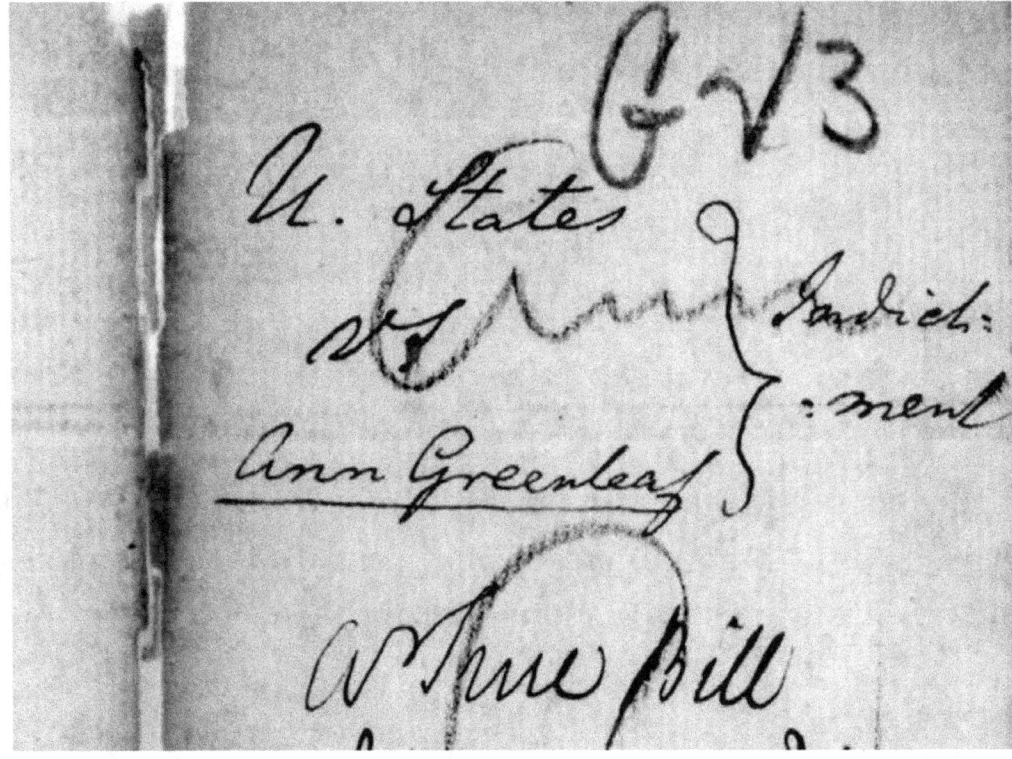

Though freedom of the press was protected in the First Amendment, its application would be tested just a few years later when political parties developed in the mid-1790s. As politicians split into Federalists (such as Alexander Hamilton and John Adams) and Democratic-Republicans (like Thomas Jefferson and James Madison), newspapers sprouted up supporting the opinions of one side or the other.

Background

Greenleaf's New Daily Advertiser, published by Ann Greenleaf, was one of the divisive papers that emerged when the early American political camps of the Federalists and Democratic-Republicans formed. It frequently opposed the decisions of the party in power: the Federalists. Ann Greenleaf was one of 25 people (all expressing anti-Federalist opinions) who was arrested for violating the Sedition Act. This bill made it a crime, punishable by two years in jail and a $2,000 fine, to "print, utter, or publish...any false, scandalous, and malicious writing" against any part of the Government.

In the February 9, 1799 issue, Greenleaf published an article that questioned the constitutionality of the Alien and Sedition Acts. The article described citizens of Flat Bush (in what is now Brooklyn, N.Y.) erecting liberty poles as they had done prior to the American Revolution to show displeasure toward the British. The cause of their current displeasure was the recent passing of what the paper called the "Tyrannical and Unconstitutional Alien and Sedition Bills." With the Sedition Act in place, Greenleaf was indicted for exciting the "Hatred of the good People of the United States" against Congress.

She was also indicted for publishing an article the following August that asserted that Pro-Federalist newspapers were both employed in the service of the U.S. Government and secret agents of the British government "sent here to assist in demoralizing the Political mind." The article based its assertion on the fact that these papers (like Noah Webster's *American Minerva*) were excessively pro-British and bitterly anti-French.

In the end, Ann Greenleaf's case would never go to trial. Since she had sold her paper and was no longer in publishing, the U.S. Attorney for the NY District recommended to President John Adams that the Government drop its case; Adams agreed.

Think About

How did the Sedition Act passed by Congress in the summer of 1798 limit freedom of the press?

Analyze the Document

Consider the following questions as you look at the court case indictment on the next pages:

- How does the indictment describe Ann Greenleaf and the crimes she committed?

- Why do you think phrases such as "wicked, malicious and seditious person" and "wickedly and maliciously intending and contriving to defame the Government...excite the Hatred of the good People of the United States" were used?

- Focus your attention on the selections quoted from the February and August issues of *Greenleaf's New Daily Advertiser*. The quote from the February issue begins near the bottom of the first page with "It appears that the Honest Yeomanry..." The selection from the August issue begins one-third of the way through the third page with "To say those principles have crept into our public counsels...":

  - What arguments do the selections from Greenleaf's New Daily Advertiser make about the Federal government?

  - In the text before these *Greenleaf's New Daily Advertiser* selections, how does the indictment describe the result of publishing these articles?

Document

The following pages are the indictment of Ann Greenleaf from the court case *United States* v. *Ann Greenleaf*. A transcription follows each page.

New York ss: The Jurors of the United States of America for the New York District in the Eastern Circuit upon their Oaths present that Ann Greenleaf of the City of New York in the New York District Widow, being a wicked Malicious and seditious Person and wickedly and Maliciously intending and contriving to defame the Government of the United States, and to excite the Hatred of the good People of the United States against the Congress of the United States and to stir up sedition within the said United States and to insinuate and cause it to be believed that the said Congress had passed tyrannical and unconstitutional Laws and were inimical to the Liberties of the said People on the ninth day of February in the Year of our Lord one thousand seven hundred and ninety nine with Force and Arms at the City of New York in the New York District wickedly Maliciously and unlawfully printed uttered and published, and caused and procured to be printed, uttered and published in a certain News Paper called "Greenleaf's New Daily Advertiser" a certain False Scandalous and Malicious writing against the Government of the United States and against the Congress of the United States in which said writing are contained among other things divers false scandalous and Malicious Matters according to the effect following that is to say. It appears that the Honest Yeomanry of that Town (a certain Town called Flat Bush meaning) some days before erected a Liberty Pole, what was common to be done at the commencement of the American Revolution

Transcription

(Italics indicate selections quoted from *Greenleaf's New Daily Advertiser*.)

New York [illegible]: The jurors of the United States of America for the New York District in the Eastern Circuit upon their oaths present that Ann Greenleaf of the City of New York in the New York District widow, being a wicked, malicious and seditious person and wickedly and maliciously intending and contriving to defame the government of the United States, and to excite the Hatred of the good people of the United States against the Congress of the United States and to stir up sedition within the said United States and to insinuate and cause it to be believed that the said Congress had passed, tyrannical and unconstitutional Laws and were inimical to the Liberties of the said People on the ninth day of February in the Year of our Lord one thousand seven hundred and ninety nine with Force and Arms at the City of New York in the New York district wickedly maliciously and unlawfully printed uttered and published, and caused and procured to be printed, uttered and published in a certain newspaper called "Greenleafs New Daily Advertiser" a certain False Scandalous and malicious writing against the Government of the United States and against the Congress of the United States in which said writing are contained among other things divers false, scandalous and malicious matters according to the effect following that is to say. *It appears that the Honest Yeomanry of that Town (a certain Town called Flat Bush meaning) some days before erected a Liberty Pole, what was common to be done at the commencement of the American Revolution* in every Republican Town in America, evincing their Marked disapprobation of British attempts to bind them in all cases whatsoever and at present expressive of the high displeasure of that Town (the said Town of Flat Bush meaning) at similar attempts in their Opinion in the last session of Congress (the then last session of Congress meaning) manifested by actually passing the tyrannical and unconstitutional alien and sedition Bills, (meaning two certaining acts of Congress commonly called by those Names the first being the act entitled "an act concerning aliens" and the other the Act entitled "an act in addition to the act entitled act for the punishment of certain crimes against the United States," in open violation of the laws of the United States, to the evil and pernicious example of all others in the like case offending, against the form of the Statute in such case thereof made and provided and against the peace of the United States and their dignity. And the Jurors aforesaid upon their Oaths aforesaid do further Present that the said Ann Greenleaf being such Person as aforesaid, and again unlawfully, wickedly and Maliciously and seditiously devising, contriving and intending to defame the Government of the United States, to stir up sedition within the said States, and to bring the said Government into hatred and contempt and to insinuate and cause it to be believed that the said Government was corrupt and inimical to the preservation of civil Liberty and to the Spirit and Principle of the Constitution of the said States, afterwards to wit, on the thirty first day of August in

Transcription

(Italics indicate selections quoted from *Greenleaf's New Daily Advertiser*.)

in every Republican Town in America, evincing their Marked disapprobation of British attempts to bind them in all cases whatsoever and at present is oppressive of the high displeasure of that Town (the said Town of Flat Bush meaning) *at similar attempts in their Opinion in the last session of Congress* (the then last session of Congress meaning) *manifested by actually passing the Tyrannical and unconstitutional alien and sedition Bills,* (meaning two certain acts of Congress commonly called by those Names the first being the act entitled "an act concerning aliens," and the other the Act entitled "an act in addition to the act entitled act for the punishment of certain crimes against the United States") in open violation of the laws of the United States, to the evil and pernicious example of all others in the like case offending, against the form of the Statute in such case thereof made and provided and against the peace of the United States and their Dignity. And the jurors aforesaid upon their Oaths aforesaid do further Present that the said Ann Greenleaf being such Person as aforesaid, and again unlawfully, wickedly maliciously and seditious by devising, continuing and intending to defame the Government of the United States and to stir up sedition within the said States, and to bring the said Government into Hatred and contempt and to insinuate and cause it to be believed that the said Government was corrupt and inimical to the preservation of civil Liberty and to the spirit and principle of the Constitution of the said States, afterwards, to wit, on the thirty first day of August in

the Year of our Lord one thousand seven hundred and ninety nine with Force and Arms at the City of NewYork in the NewYork District wickedly maliciously and unlawfully printed uttered and published and caused and procured to be printed uttered and published in a certain News Paper called Greenleafs New Daily Advertiser a certain other false scandalous and Malicious writing against the government of the said States in which said last mentioned writing are contained amongst other things divers false, scandalous and malicious matters according to the effect following that is to say "to say those principles have crept into our pub-
"lic councils, to say that public servants advocate and
"forward this gradual subversion of National Charac-
"ter, this insidious revolution of sentiment, would per-
"haps be construed into sedition. But thank God in
"this Country truth is not yet a libel, and I may
"still assert facts, that are too prominent to be done
"away by legal sophistry, or federal assertion.
"1. A News Paper in Boston — Noah Webster in New-
"York — the Farmers Weekly Museum in New Hamp-
"shire — Fenno in Philadelphia — and Youngland
"Browns paper in Baltimore, are pensioned and still
"in the pay of Government.
"2. All those presses continually nauseate us with
"Eulogiums on the British; publish nothing but the
"most severe Philippicks against the French, and
"sedulously suppress every transaction, that tends to
"give the publick an idea of the infamous conduct
"of the British towards our Commerce and our Citizens

Transcription

(Italics indicate selections quoted from *Greenleaf's New Daily Advertiser*.)

the Year of our Lord one thousand seven hundred and ninety nine with Force and Arms at the City of New York in the New York District wickedly, maliciously and unlawfully printed uttered and published and caused and procured to the be printed uttered and published in a certain News Paper called "Greeleafs New Daily Advertiser" a certain other false scandalous and malicious writing against the Government of the said States in which said last mentioned writing are contained among other things divers false, scandalous and malicious matters according to the effect following that is to say *"To say those principles have crept into our public councils, to say that public servants advocate and forward this gradual subversion of the National Character, this insiduous revolution of sentiment, would perhaps be construed into sedition. But thank God in this Country truth is not yet a libel, and I may still assert facts, that are too prominent to be done away by legal sophistry, or federal assertion.*

1. A News Paper in Boston- Noah Websters in New York—the Famous Weekly Muwseum in New Hampshire—Fonnor's in Philadelphia- and Yundtand Brown's paper in Baltimore, are pensioned and held in the pay of Government.

2. All those Presses continually nauseate us with Eulogiums on the British; publish nothing but the most severe Philippricks against the French, and sedulously suppress every transaction, that tends to give the publick an idea of the infamous conduct of the British towards our Commerce and our Citizens

"3 These papers are celebrated for writing the basest per-
"sonal scurrility against every individual particular-
"ly, Editors that wish to keep alive that jealousy and
"watchfulness so essential to the preservation of civil Li-
"berty — and endeavour to preserve the Spirit and
"Principles of our Constitution in its pristine purity.
"4. Is it not probable that these pensioned Printers
"have their directions from their Masters or that they
"anticipate and exercise their pleasure?
"5. Is it not probable that writers are hired for the
"Assistance of such Editors as are incapable of writing
"themselves, such as little Brown for instance, and
"others of the same stamp; and that these ven-
"al scribblers may be British secret agents, sent here
"to assist in demoralizing the Political mind.
"Last year the British secret service money, exceeded the
"amount of a whole years expences of our Government.
"But who can tell thro' what channel it was expen-
"ded — the British notwithstanding their great hu-
"manity and their mighty Generosity, are seldom
"known to give something for nothing. And who that
"witnesses the conduct of federal prints, who that
"observes their Partialities for that Nation,
"but must entertain their own suspicions.
"These Observations are not the ebullition of party fever
" they have the most certain truths for their basis,
"and deserve the utmost attention from every friend
"to the Independence, Respectability and happiness
"of his country" in open violation of the Laws of the
United States, to the Evil and pernicious example
of all others in the like case offending, against the

Transcription

(Italics indicate selections quoted from *Greenleaf's New Daily Advertiser*.)

3. These papers are celebrated for venting the basest personal scurrility against every individual particularly, Editors, that wish to keep alive that jealousy and watchfulness so essential to the preservation of civil Liberty—and endeavor to preserve the spirit and principles of our Constitution in its pristine purity.

4. Is it not probable that these pensioned Printers have their directions from their Masters, or that they anticipate and exercise their pleasure?

5. Is it not probable that writers are hired for the Assistance of such Editors as are incapable of writing themselves, such as little Brown for instance, and others of the same stamp; and that these venal scriblers may be British secret agents sent here to assist in demoralizing the Political mind. Last year the British secret service money exceeded the amount of a whole years expences of our Government. But who can tell thro what channel it was expended – the British notwithstanding then Great humanity and their mighty Generosity, are seldom known to give something for nothing. And who that witnesses the Conduct of federal prints, who that observes their Partiality for that Nation, but must entertain their own suspicions. These Observations are not the ebullition of party favor they have the most certain Truths for their basis, and deserve the utmost attention from every friend to the Independence, Respectability and happiness of his Country" in open violation of the Laws of the United States, to the Evil and pernicious Example of all others in the like case offending, against the form of the Statute in such case thereof made and provided and against the peace of the said United States and their Dignity.

Transcription

Form of the Statute in such case thereof made and provided and against the peace of the said United States and their Dignity.

Discuss

- Read Section 2 of the Sedition Act at https://www.ourdocuments.gov/doc.php?flash=true&doc=16&page=transcript#no-3 — how did the provided selections from *Greenleaf's New Daily Advertiser* violate the law?

- Do you think the Sedition Act was constitutional?

- How does the criticism leveled at Congress and the Government compare to criticisms that the media makes today?

Permission to "Take it to the Streets"

The right of the people to peaceably assemble is guaranteed in the Bill of Rights, in the First Amendment to the Constitution. But what happens when a city requires a group to obtain a permit to do so?

Background

The 1968 Democratic National Convention is associated in the minds of many with scenes of violent clashes between anti-war protestors and Chicago police officers. Yet the National Mobilization Committee to End the War in Vietnam's (MOBE) application for a permit highlights the protestors' desire to abide by municipal (local government) regulations while exercising their First Amendment rights.

The application was an exhibit in criminal case 69CR180, *United States* v. *Dellinger, et al*. The defendants, David Dellinger, Rennie Davis, Tom Hayden, Abbie Hoffman, Jerry Rubin, Lee Weiner, John Froines, and Bobby Seale, were accused of inciting riots during the Convention. On March 20, 1969, the grand jury returned indictments on these eight people on charges of conspiracy to travel in interstate commerce with the intent to incite a riot, in violation of the Anti-Riot Act. Six of the defendants were indicted on individual charges. After a 13-month trial, Judge Hoffman sentenced Bobby Seale to four years in prison for contempt of court and declared a mistrial in the prosecution of Seale.

Think About

Should a local government be able to regulate the American right to peaceably assemble, as guaranteed by the First Amendment. If so, how?

Analyze the Document

Consider the following questions as you look at the permit application on the next pages:

- Who submitted the application?

- When was it submitted?

- How many participants were expected?

- How many different departments needed to approve a permit application?

Document

The following page is a permit application that the National Mobilization Committee to End the War in Vietnam (MOBE) submitted to the City of Chicago for approval to march on public streets during the 1968 Democratic National Convention.

Exhibit A

CITY OF CHICAGO
DEPARTMENT OF STREETS AND SANITATION
APPLICATION ONLY - NOT A PERMIT

Application No. ____

Date July 25, 1968

APPLICATION FOR PERMIT - SPECIAL EVENT USING THE PUBLIC WAY
(For explanations - see reverse side)

IT IS REQUIRED THAT THIS APPLICATION BE MADE AT LEAST 30 DAYS PRIOR TO THE EVENT

Application is hereby made for Permit to use public way as hereinafter described at location herein designated.

1. To be issued to: Name _National Mobilization Committee To End the War in Vietnam_
   Address _Room 315, 407 S. Dearborn, Chicago, Illinois_
2. Name and Telephone Number of Person to Contact _Rennie Davis   939-2666_
3. Type of activity (check one) [X] Parade [ ] Motorcade [ ] Assembly [ ] Other (describe) ____
4. Inclusive dates and times of activity _August 28, 1968   11:00 am - 4:00 pm_
5. Description of activity - if Parade give: (a) Assembly Area; (b) Exact Route; (c) Disbanding Area - (d) Estimate of number of vehicles, marchers, etc., that will participate.

   (a) _Wacker Drive; State St on the East, Wacker Dr on the West. (b) State Street South to Jackson Blvd, East to Columbus Drive, South to Grant Park bandshell (c) Grant Park Band Shell (d) 150,000 marchers_

NOTE: This application will be considered by the Parade Board at its next regular meeting. You will be notified by mail as to date, time, and place, if it is deemed necessary that a representative of your organization be present.

By _Rennie Davis_   Title _Project Director, National Mobil._
   Authorized representative (Signature)

Mail to: Department of Streets and Sanitation - Att'n: Chairman Parade Board
Room 707 - City Hall, Chicago 2, Illinois

THIS SPACE BELOW IS FOR USE BY THE CITY OF CHICAGO

Approved/Disapproved by Dept. of Streets and Sanitation ____
Approved/Disapproved by Dept. of Police ____
Approved/Disapproved by Chicago Transit Authority ____
Approved/Disapproved by Chicago Park District ____
Approved by Commissioner of Streets and Sanitation ____
Noted - Board of Underground ____

(Amendments and Changes by the Parade Board will be noted on Reverse Side.)

A

Discuss

- Why would the City of Chicago be opposed to granting a permit to MOBE for Wednesday, August 28, 1968?

- If the City of Chicago denied MOBE a permit to assemble, what should MOBE Project Director Rennie Davis have done?

- Do you think obtaining a permit hinders one's right to peaceably assemble?

A Seditious Petition

The right to petition the government is protected by the First Amendment. Less than 10 years after its ratification, however, a New York State legislator was arrested for distributing a petition. His petition, addressed to the House and Senate, questioned recent government actions stating that Congress had just deliberately passed a "series of Evils" that would lead to a "foreign war, a violated Constitution and a divided People."

Background

Revolutionary War veteran Jedediah Peck served as judge for a New York State court and was elected to the N.Y. state legislature as a Federalist. He, however, disagreed with the Federalist's passage of the Alien and Sedition Acts that increased the requirements for citizenship and limited freedom of expression respectively.

So, in April 1799 he asserted his First Amendment right to "petition the Government for a redress of grievances." For distributing this petition, and the specific language that it used, Jedediah Peck (an elected representative) was one of 25 people arrested for violating the Sedition Act.

Affidavits from witnesses described him carrying a six-inch stack of handbills with him and telling others that Congress was threatening the liberties of the United States. The indictment also describes the language of the petition to the House and Senate as containing "false, scandalous and malicious writings." Among other claims, Peck was arrested for attacking the Alien and Sedition Acts and saying they were "obnoxious to a generous and free people" and so wicked that they'd "convert Freemen into Slaves."

Jedediah Peck was arrested, and subject to two years in jail and a $2,000 fine. He never went to trial, however, since the U.S. Attorney (after reaching out to the Secretary of State and President John Adams himself) decided not to pursue the case. For Jedediah Peck, his controversial statements helped gain him support — he was re-elected to the N.Y. state legislature. Today he is credited by some as the father of the N.Y. public school system.

Think About

How did the Sedition Act passed by Congress on July 14, 1798 aim to limit freedom to petition?

Analyze the Document

Consider the following questions as you look at the court case indictment on the next pages:

- How does the indictment describe Jedediah Peck and his crime?

- In the quoted selections from his petition, how does Peck describe the French government and the Adams administration's interactions?

- In the quoted selections, how does Peck describe the Alien and Sedition Act?

Document

The following pages are the indictment of Jedediah Peck in the court case *United States* v. *Jedediah Peck*. A transcription follows each page.

New York ss: The Jurors for the United States of America for the New York District in the Eastern Circuit upon their Oath present that Jedidiah Peck of the Town of Burlington in the County of Otsego in the New York District Esquire being a wicked seditious and ill disposed Person, and wickedly and maliciously intending and contriving to defame the Government of the said United States, and the Congress thereof, and to stir up Sedition within the said United States, and to excite the Hatred of the good People of the said States against the said Government and Congress, on the fifteenth Day of April in the Year of our Lord one thousand seven hundred and ninety nine with Force and Arms at the Town of Otsego in the County of Otsego in the New York District wickedly maliciously and unlawfully uttered and published, and caused and procured to be uttered and published and aided and assisted in uttering & publishing a certain false scandalous and malicious Writing against the Government of the United States, & against the Congress and President of the said States, addressed to the Senate and Representatives of the United States in Congress assembled, in which said

Transcription

New York [illegible]: The jurors for the United States of America for the NewYork District in the Eastern Circuit upon their Oath present that Jedediah Peck of the Town of Burlington in the County of Otsego in the New York district Esquire being a wicked seditious and ill disposed Person, and wickedly and maliciously in tending and contriving to defame the Government of the said United States, and the Congress thereof, and to stir up sedition within the said United States, and to excite the Hatred of the good People of the said States against the said Government and Congress, on the Fifteenth Day of April in the Year of our Lord one thousand seven hundred and ninety nine with, Force and Arms at the Town of Otsego in the County of Otsego in the New York District wickedly maliciously and unlawfully uttered and published, and caused and procured to be uttered and published and aided and assisted in uttering & publishing a certain false scandalous and malicious Writing against the Government of the United States, & against the Congress and President of the said States, addressed to the Senate and Representatives of the United States in Congress assembled, in which said

said Writing are contained among other Things divers false, scandalous & malicious Matters according to the Effect following, to wit, "To our Minds, under the purest and most deliberate Exercise, they (the Measures of Congress meaning) present instead of Objects of Exultation or Complacency, Applause or Approbation, a Series of Evils equally diffusive and calamitous, equally general and destructive - a foreign War, a violated Constitution and a divided People" and also divers other false scandalous and malicious Matters according to the Effect following, that is to say, "But when we find Declarations thus open & explicit (meaning certain Declarations of the Minister of the French Republic for foreign Affairs stated in the said Writing) accompanied by Acts of substantial Justice, we should betray a miserable Jealousy or criminal Scepticism were we to join the Administration (meaning the President and principal Officers concerned in administring the Government of the said United States) in concluding that we can discover in the French Government only empty Professions of a Desire to conciliate. So far from this we percieve in their Acts (the Acts of the French Government meaning) an Approach to Accomodation, which if met on our Part with similar Dispositions might soon revive the Cordiality and Intercourse which ever ou

Transcription

(Italics indicate selections quoted from Jedediah Peck's petition.)

said Writing are contained among other Things divers false, scandalous & malicious matters according to the Effect following, to wit, *"To our minds, under the purest and most deliberate Exercise, they (the measures of Congress meaning) present instead of Objects of Exultation or Complacency, Applause or Approbation a Series of Evils equally diffusive and calamitous, equally general and destructive – a foreign war, a violated Constitution and a divided People"* and also divers other false scandalous and malicious matters according to the Effect following, that is to say, *"But when we find Declarations thus open & explicit (meaning certain Declarations of the Minister of the French Republic for foreign affairs stated in the said writing) accompanied by Acts of substantial Justice, we should betray a miserable jealousy or criminal scepticism were we to join the Administration (meaning the President and principal officers concerned in administering the Government of the said United States) in concluding that we can discover in the French Government only empty Professions of a Desire to conciliate. So far from this we perceive in their Acts (The Acts of the French government meaning) an approach to accommodation, which if met on our Part with similar Dispositions might soon revive the cordiality and intercourse which ever [illegible]*

to exist between two People mutually profess:
:sing an Attachment to Peace & mutually ac:
:knowledging it's Wisdom and Virtue. It is
therefore with the deepest Concern that
we find Measures originating in Mistake
and prosecuted in Error, become the Foun:
:dation of a System of Alarm, of Suspicion,
of Tyranny, and of Expence (meaning to
insinuate that the Measures of the said
Government of the United States were a System of Alarm, of
Suspicion, of Tyranny, and of unjustifiable
Expence) which no State of Things could
justify, and scarcely any extenuate" —
and in which said Writing are also con:
:tained divers other false, scandalous &
malicious Matters to the Effect following
that is to say "The Parts of this System
(the said Measures of the Government of
the United States meaning) which most
immediately engage our Attention, and
to which we are most desirous of directing
yours, are the two Laws, passed at your
last Session (the then last Session of the
said Congress meaning) usually deno:
:minated the Alien and Sedition Laws
and an Act providing for the Augmen:
:tation of the Army. The first of these
Laws (a certain Act of the said Congress
entitled "An Act concerning Aliens" meaning)
has all the Characters which can make it
obnoxious to a generous and free People.
It is cruel, unjust, unnecessary, impolitic
and unconstitutional" — And in which said
Writing are also contained divers other
false scandalous and malicious Matters
to the Effect following that is to say "To
the Sedition Law (a certain Act of the said
Congress

Transcription

(Italics indicate selections quoted from Jedediah Peck's petition.)

to exist between two people mutually professing an attachment to Peace & mutually acknowledging its freedom and virtue. It is therefore with the deepest concern that we find measures originating in [illegible] and prosecuted in [illegible], become the foundation of a system of alarm, of suspicion of Tyranny, and of Expence (meaning to insinuate that the measures of the said Government of the United States were a system of alarm, of suspicion, of Tyranny, and of unjustifiable Expense) *which no state of things could justify, and scarcely any extenuate"* - and in which said writing [illegible] also contained divers other false, scandalous & malicious Matters to the Effect following that is to say *"The parts of this System* (the said measures of the Government of the United States meaning) *which most immediately engage our attention, and to which we are most desirous of directing yours, are the two Laws, passed at your last session* (the then last session of the said Congress meaning) *usually denominated the Alien and Sedition Laws and Act providing for the Augmentation of the Army - The first of these Laws* (a certain Act of the said Congress entitled "An act concerning Aliens" meaning *how all the characters which can make it obnoxious to a generous and free People. It is cruel, unjust, unnecessary, impolitic and unconstitutional"* – And in which said writing are also contained divers other false scandalous and malicious matters to the Effect following that is to say, *"To the Sedition Law* (a certain Act of the said Congress

Congress entitled "An Act in Addition to the Act intituled An Act for the Punishment of certain Crimes against the United States, meaning) our Objections are still stronger than to the Alien Law, because the Abuses to which it is liable, are equally vicious in their Character, and more general in their Operation. The former assails the few, the latter attacks the many. The former is directed at Foreigners; the latter is levelled at ourselves. The former tyrannizes over Men, who in general have been born and bred under Oppression. But it is the superlative Wickedness of the latter to convert Freemen into Slaves."— And in which said Writing are also contained divers other false scandalous and malicious Matters according to the Effect following "But it is not on this Ground alone that we think the late Augmentation of the Army (the Army of the said United States meaning) unnecessary. The Law creating it is predicated upon a Declaration of War against the United States, an actual Invasion of their Territory, or an imminent Danger of such Invasion discovered in the Opinion of the President to exist. That any Declaration of War against the United States, or any actual Invasion of their Territory does exist, will not be pretended. It follows then that this Law is put into Operation from some imminent Danger of Invasion discovered in the Opinion of the President to exist. But from what Quarter is such Invasion to be expected? Is it from a Nation who
Ruler.

Transcription

(Italics indicate selections quoted from Jedediah Peck's petition.)

Congress entitled "An act in Addition to the Act entitled An Act for the Punishment of certain crimes against the United States meaning) our Objections are still stronger than to the Alien Laws, because the abuses to which it is liable, are equally vicious in their Character, and more general in their Operation. The former assails the few, the latter attacks the many. The former is directed as Foreigners; the latter is leveled as ourselves. The former tyrannizes over men, who in general have been born and bred under oppression. But it is the superlative Wickedness of the latter to convert Freeman into Slave." – And in which said Writing are also contained divers other false scandalous and malicious matters according to the Effect following *"But it is not or this ground alone that we think the late augmentation of the Army (the Army of the said United States meaning) unnecessary. The Law executing it is predicated upon a Declaration of War against the United States, an actual Invasion of their Territory, or an imminent danger of each Invasion discovered in the Opinion of the President to exist. That any Declaration of War against the United States, or any actual invasion of their Territory does exist will not be pretended. It follows then that this Law is put into operation from some imminent Danger of Invasion discovered in the opinion of the President to exist. But from what quarter is such invasion to be expected? It is from a nation wh[illegible - cut off] Ruler.*

Rulers declare themselves anxious for Reconciliation? A nation already exhausted by Defeat? A nation, whose Ports are all in a state of Blockade? A nation, which the most confidential Servant of the Cabinet informs us, will not, in the short Period of two additional Years, have a single Ship afloat upon the Ocean? A nation wasting itself in barren Conquests on the opposite side of the Globe? A nation on the Eve of a new Rupture with the great continental Powers of Europe? A nation in short which can no longer attach her own Subjects, nor controul her own Dependencies? Is it from a People th impotent and embarassed that we have to dread an Invasion? It is impossible; they are the Fears of Dotage, or Circumspection of Cowardice, and merit only Pity or Contempt". all which false scandalous & malicious Matters & the said writing containing the same were so as aforesaid uttered and published, & caused and procured to be uttered and published & the said Jedediah Peck did so as aforesaid aid and assist in uttering & publishing the same in open Violation of the Laws of the United States, to the evil & pernicious Example of all others in the like Case offending, against the Form of the Statute in such Case thereof made & provided, and against the Peace of the said United States & their Dignity.

Transcription

(Italics indicate selections quoted from Jedediah Peck's petition.)

Rulers declare themselves anxious for Reconciliation? A Nation already exhausted by defeat? A Nation, whose ports are all a state of Blockade? A Nation, which the most confidential Servant of the Cabinet informs us, will not, in the short period of two additional years, have a single ship afloat upon the Ocean? A Nation wasting itself in barren conquests on the opposite side of the Globe? A Nation on the Eve of a new Rupture with the great continental Powers of Europe? A Nation in short which can no longer attack her own subjects, nor control her own Dependencies? Is it from a People this impotent and embarrassed that we have to dread an Invasion? It is impossible; they are the Fears of Dotage, or Circumspection of Cowardice, and merit only Pity or Contempt" - all which false scandalous & malicious matters & the said writing containing the same were so as aforesaid uttered and published, & caused and procured to be uttered and published & the said Jedediah Peck did so as aforesaid aid and assist in uttering & publishing the same in open Violation of the Laws of the United States, to the evil & pernicious example of all others in the like Case offending, against the Form of the Statute in such Case thereof made & provided, and against the Peace of the said United States & their Dignity.

Discuss

- Read Section 2 of the Sedition Act at https://www.ourdocuments.gov/doc.php?flash=true&doc=16&page=transcript#no-3 — did Jedediah Peck violate the law? Why or why not?

- Do you think the Sedition Act was constitutional?

- How would our nation be different if the Sedition act was still in effect? What would the consequences be?

Examining the Second Amendment

The Second Amendment to the U.S. Constitution is controversial and polarizes American public opinion. It says: "A well regulated Militia, being necessary to the security of a free State, the right of the people to keep and bear Arms, shall not be infringed."

Background

The Second Amendment can be considered in two parts: "a well regulated militia" and "the right of the people to keep and bear arms."

The Founders were distrustful of a professional "standing army" and were adamant that the United States military be a volunteer organization (called a militia) that was ultimately controlled by civilian authority. This is why the President of the United States is the Commander in Chief and Congress must approve declarations of war. This concern can be seen in many letters, articles and other documents.

John Adams's 1763 "Essay on Man's Lust for Power" (http://founders.archives.gov/documents/Adams/06-01-02-0045-0008) says:

> Power is a Thing of infinite Danger and Delicacy, and was never yet confided to any Man or any Body of Men without turning their Heads.— Was there ever, in any Nation or Country, since the fall, a standing Army that was not carefully watched and controuled by the State so as to keep them impotent, that did not, ravish, plunder, Massacre and ruin, and at last inextricably inslave the People…

A 1770 letter to Benjamin Franklin from the Massachusetts House of Representatives (http://founders.archives.gov/documents/Franklin/01-17-02-0165) states:

> … So wretched is the State of this Province, not only to be subjected to absolute Instructions given to the Governor to be the Rule of his Administration, whereby some of the most essential Clauses of our Charter vesting in him Powers to be exercised for the Good of the People are totally rescinded, which is in reality a State of Despotism; but also to a Standing Army, which being uncontrouled by any Authority in the Province, must soon tear up the very Foundation of civil Government.

The Declaration of Independence (https://www.archives.gov/founding-docs/declaration/what-does-it-say) reads:

> He has kept among us, in times of peace, Standing Armies without the Consent of our legislatures.
>
> He has affected to render the Military independent of and superior to the Civil power.

A 1787 letter from Thomas Jefferson to James Madison, Secretary of State, during the Constitutional Convention (http://founders.archives.gov/documents/Jefferson/01-12-02-0454) reads:

> ...I will now add what I do not like. First the omission of a bill of rights providing clearly and without the aid of sophisms for freedom of religion, freedom of the press, protection against standing armies, restriction against monopolies, the eternal and unremitting force of the habeas corpus laws, and trials by jury in all matters of fact triable by the laws of the land and not by the law of Nations...

New York's ratification of the U.S. Constitution (with proposed amendments) from 1788 (https://catalog.archives.gov/id/24278854) says:

> That the People have the right to keep and bear arms; that a well-regulated Militia, including the body of the People capable of bearing arms, is the proper, natural and safe defense of a Free State; that the Militia should not be subject to martial law, except in times of War, Rebellion, and Insurrection.
>
> That standing Armies in time of peace are dangerous to Liberty, and ought not to be kept up, except in Cases of necessity; and that at all times the Military should be under strict subordination to the civil Power.

And the 1859 Kansas Territory Wyandotte Constitution, what later became the Kansas State Constitution, (https://www.docsteach.org/documents/document/wyandot-constitution) says:

The people have the right to bear arms for their defense and security, but standing armies, in time of peace, are dangerous to liberty, and shall not be tolerated, and the military shall be in strict subordination to the civil power. The Founders considered the right to keep and bear arms primarily for the purpose of "defense and security." After all, before and during the Revolutionary War the people of the United States had been attacked by standing, professional armies without "due process of law" at the discretion of officers without civilian oversight. Also, weapons were a necessity for protection against predators and unknown dangers on the ever-expanding frontier.

Over time, however, laws have been passed to protect the public from dangers associated with expanding technology and weapons falling into the wrong hands:

- The National Firearms Act of 1934 imposed a substantial tax on automatic-fire weapons and what were seen as gangster-related weapons, like sawed-off shotguns and guns hidden in canes.
- The Federal Firearms Act of 1938 required licenses and record-keeping for all gun sales and prohibited sales to known criminals.
- The Gun Control Act of 1968 increased restrictions on known criminals and outlawed mail-order sales of rifles and shotguns.
- The Law Enforcement Officers Protection Act of 1986 banned armor-piercing ammunition.
- The Firearm Owners Protection Act of 1986 eased restrictions on the sale of some guns, but raised penalties for certain crimes involving guns.
- The Crime Control Act of 1990 raised criminal penalties for possessing and discharging firearms in a school zone.

- The Brady Handgun Violence Protection Act of 1994 led to the creation of the National Instant Criminal Background Check System.
- The Violent Crime Control and Law Enforcement Act of 1994 included the Federal Assault Weapons Ban.

Think About

- Why do Americans interpret the wording in the Second Amendment differently?

- How long has the controversy surrounding its interpretation been going on?

Analyze the Documents

Consider the following questions as you look at the two letters about the right to bear arms on the next pages:

- When were these letters sent?

- Who were they sent to?

- What does each of the authors want?

- What arguments do they present to back up their opinions?

Document

The following pages are a letter from J. M. Blough to the National Law Enforcement Commission, and an enclosed cover from "Short Stories" magazine containing articles which romanticize guns, according to Mr. Blough. Blough requests legislation to restrict the purchase of firearms.

1309 Franklin St.,
Johnstown, Pa.,
Sept. 10, 1929.

The National Law Enforcement Commission,
Washington, D. C.

RECEIVED
SEP 1... 1929
NATIONAL COMMISSION ON LAW
OBSERVANCE AND ENFORCEMENT

Gentlemen:

I understand that a committee has been appointed to study the cause of crime. This is very important indeed. For their consideration I beg to present a few things:

1. I enclose the front cover page of one copy of "Short Stories". I consider such pictures in our magazines and such stories which constantly tell of shooting and other crimes as a most prolific source of crime, for the young folks who see them and read them are inspired to do the same.

2. Moving Pictures are another source of crime. This has been proven again and again. For in many moving pictures crime is displayed and often the hero is guilty of crime himself, and so children are led to believe it is smart to commit a crime and often the proper thing to do.

These are two main causes of crime which could be largely eliminated by the following legislation:

All pictures of crime are prohibited on the screen, advertising posters, magazines and newspapers, etc.

All stories told so as to condone crime or praise it should be positively forbidden.

3. The ease with which people in America can buy firearms and ammunition is the <u>greatest</u> cause of crime in America. Why should every one indiscriminately be allowed to have a weapon?

I have lived for 25 years in India and with that large population we do not have as many crimes in a year as some of our cities have in a month. Why is it? Because/ the sale of firearms is restricted. No one can buy a weapon or ammunition without a license from the Government, neither can he sell it to some one else . In this way the Gov. knows exactly how many people have firearms and who they are. Every year a check is made of all of them. If any one is found guilty of misusing his privilege to own a weapon his license is revoked and the weapon is taken from him. Only decent and trustworthy people can secure a license, and then only if they can show sufficient reason why they should have the permission.

Until the U.S. passes some law similar to this we cannot hope to reduce crime in America materially. Most crimes are committed by shooting, and the most wicked criminal can always secure a weapon. There is no constraint.

I recommend to you these three causes for your consideration, and trust you may urge legislation to curb these evils.

Very sincerely yours,

J. M. Blough.

A Novel of Railroad Gunmen by Chas. W. Tyler

Short Stories
Twice A Month

JULY 10th 25¢

30c in Canada

WILLIAM MACLEOD RAINE'S
NEW NOVEL BEGINS WITH HUMMING LEAD!

The Fighting Tenderfoot
Looks for Trouble

Document

The following page is a letter sent by Charles Koch to Congress in 1975 opposing all laws limiting individual gun ownership, but expressing support for mandatory sentencing for criminals who use guns.

PUNISH CRIMINALS NOT GUNS

Charles Koch
Rt 3 Box 32A
Floresville, Texas
78114

DEC 3 1970

Dear Congressmen:,

I want to voice my strong opposition to all gun control laws.

I do support mandatory jail sentences for all criminals who use firearms.

Sincerely
Charles Koch

WHAT THE CONSTITUTION SAYS ABOUT FIREARMS

"A well regulated Militia, being necessary to the security of a free State, the right of the people to keep and bear Arms shall not be infringed." 2nd Amendment

CONSTITUTIONAL RIGHT

TO OWN AND BEAR ARMS

THE RIGHT TO BEAR ARMS IS AN AMERICAN HERITAGE

Discuss

- Do you think guns are romanticized like J. M. Blough suggested in his letter? How do you think how guns are portrayed in media and entertainment has changed since Blough wrote?

- How do some Americans use the wording of the Second Amendment to oppose gun control legislation?

- Do you think Americans interpret the Second Amendment differently today than it was when it was written? Do you think it should be?

Search Warrants and the Fourth Amendment

> urt for the Western Distr
>
> property so seized into
>
> fused to return to defend
>
> e (1) leather grip, value
>
> $3.00; one (1) Pettus Co

Weeks v. *The United States* was argued before the Supreme Court in 1913. The question at hand was whether the evidence seized without a search warrant was a violation of the Fourth Amendment. The Fourth Amendment says:

> The right of the people to be secure in their persons, houses, papers and effects against unreasonable searches and seizures, shall not be violated, and no warrants shall issue but upon probable cause, supported by oath or affirmation, and particularly describing the place to be searched, and the persons or things to be seized.

Background

On December 21, 1911, Fremont Weeks, an employee of the Adams Express Company, was arrested while on the job at Union Station in Kansas City, Missouri. Police suspected that Weeks was selling and "transmitting chances" in a lottery, which at the time was considered gambling, an illegal action in Missouri.

He was promptly taken to Police Station No. 4 and searched. Police officers found paper, a lead pencil, and lottery tickets. While Weeks was being held at the police station, police officers drove to his residence at a boarding house, and entered his room with help from a neighbor. They found a leather suitcase that contained mining stocks, a memo book, receipts, a wallet, and a tin box. They seized these items, without a search warrant, and turned over the evidence to the U.S. Marshal.

Officers later returned, were admitted by a boarder, and found incriminating letters written by customers placing orders for lottery tickets. Those items were seized because the law enforcement officials believed they proved that Weeks had violated federal law by using the U.S. mail to distribute lottery tickets.

Weeks was indicted on charges of gambling and using the U.S. Postal Service to distribute chances in a lottery based on this evidence. During his trial, his attorney filed a motion requesting that all evidence seized by law enforcement be returned to Weeks. He argued that the police officers and the U.S. Marshal had unlawfully, and without a search warrant, entered Weeks's home and seized property. He said the property should not be admissible during the trial.

The judge disagreed, ordering that all incriminating evidence should stay in the District Attorney's custody. Weeks was found guilty by the jury of illegal gambling, ordered to pay a $100 fine, and sentenced to six months in jail.

Immediately following sentencing, his attorney appealed the decision to the United States Supreme Court. He argued that the search was a violation of the Fourth Amendment. The Court overturned Weeks's conviction by a unanimous vote — not because he was innocent of the charges, but because the evidence that had been used to convict him had been obtained without a search warrant; it was a violation of the Fourth Amendment protecting him against unreasonable searches and seizures.

In the Court's opinion, delivered on February 24, 1914, Justice William Day further explained:

> If letters and private documents can thus be seized and held and used in evidence against a citizen accused of an offense, the protection of the Fourth Amendment, declaring his right to be secure against such searches and seizures, is of no value, and so far as those thus placed are concerned, might as well be stricken from the Constitution.

Think About

What is the value in the protection of the Fourth Amendment and being secure from illegal searches and seizures?

Analyze the Document

Consider the following questions as you look at the court case bill of exceptions on the next pages:

- How does Weeks's attorney, Martin J. O'Donnell, describe the way that police officers entered Weeks's home and seized his property? Why do you think he described it that way?

- What items did the officers take? Why do you think the attorney lists their value?

- What arguments does O'Donnell make about the evidence?

- What does he say this type of search and seizure violates?

Document

The following pages are the defendant's bill of exceptions from the court case *The United States* v. *Fremont Weeks*.

IN THE DISTRICT COURT OF THE UNITED STATES FOR THE WESTERN DIVISION
OF THE WESTERN DISTRICT OF MISSOURI.

The United States of America, Plaintiff,)
)
-vs.-) No. 3007.
)
Fremont Weeks, Defendant.)

- - - - - - - - - - - - - - - -

DEFENDANT'S BILL OF EXCEPTIONS.

BE IT REMEMBERED, that on the 7th day of November, 1912, at the regular November Term, 1912, of the District Court of the United States for the Western Division of the Western District of Missouri, at Kansas City, the above entitled cause came on to be heard before the Honorable A. S. Van Valkenburg, Judge, and a jury, and thereupon the following proceedings were had and taken, and evidence heard and offered:

APPEARANCES:

The Government appeared by Thaddeus B Landon, Esq., Assistant United States Attorney
The defendant appeared in person and by his attorney, Martin J O'Donnell, Esq.

After the Jury was sworn, and counsel for the Government and for the defendant, respectively, had addressed the Jury in opening statements, the following evidence was introduced and offered on the part of the Government:

TESTIMONY FOR THE GOVERNMENT.

MR O'DONNELL: I have filed a motion on which there has been no ruling.

THE COURT: The motion is for the return of this property.

(The motion is as follows: is in words and

PETITION TO RETURN PRIVATE PAPERS, BOOKS AND OTHER PROPERTY.

Now comes defendant and states that he is a citizen and resident

-1-

of Kansas City, Missouri, and that he resides, owns and occupies a home at 1834 Penn Street in said City;

That on the 21st day of December, 1911, while plaintiff was absent at his daily avocation certain officers of the government whose names are to plaintiff unknown, unlawfully and without warrant of authority so to do, broke open the door to plaintiff's said home and seized all of his books, letters, money, papers, notes evidences of indebtedness, stock, certificates, insurance policies, deeds, abstracts, and other muniments of title, bonds, candies, clothes and other property in said home, and this in violation of Sections 11 and 23 to the Constitution of Missouri, and of the 4th and 5th Amendments to the Constitution of the United States;

That the District Attorney, Marshal and Clerk of the United States Court for the Western District of Missouri took the above described property so seized into their possession and have failed and refused to return to defendant portion of same, to-wit:

One (1) leather grip, value of about $7.00; one (1) tin box valued at $3.00; one (1) Pettus County, Missouri, bond, value $500.00 to Three (3) mining stock certificates which defendant is unable more particularly describe valued at $12,000.00, and certain stock certificates in addition thereto issued by the San Domingo Mining Loan and Investment Company; about $75.00 in currency; one (1) newspaper published about 1790, an heirloom; and certain other property which plaintiff is now unable to describe;

That said property is being unlawfully and improperly held by said District Attorney, Marshal and Clerk in violation of defendant's rights under the Constitution of the United States and the State of Missouri;

That said District Attorney purposes to use said books, letters, papers, certificates of stock, etc., at the trial of the above entitled cause and that by reason thereof and of the facts above set forth defendant's rights under the amendments aforesaid to the Constitution of Missouri, and the United States have been and will be violated unless this Court order the return prayed for;

WHEREFORE, defendant prays that said District Attorney, Marshal, and Clerk be notified, and that the Court direct and order said District Attorney, Marshal and Clerk to return said property to said defendant.

        (signed) Martin J O'Donnell
           Attorney for Defendant.

STATE OF MISSOURI,)
) SS.
COUNTY OF JACKSON,)

      Fremont Weeks, of lawful age being duly sworn upon his oath, states that he has read the above and foregoing motion, and that the facts therein set forth are true according to his best knowledge and belief.

        (signed) Fremont Weeks

Subscribed and sworn to before me this 6th day of November, 1912.
My commission expires April 20, 1916
        Emma Powers
        Notary Public in and for Jackson County,
(L.S.)   Mo.

The Clerk will here copy into Bill of Exceptions List of Property seized and list of Property returned to defendant

THE COURT: The motion will be denied.

And to this ruling and action of the Court defendant excepted and duly saved his exception.

MR O'DONNELL: Defendant asks at this time that the Government be required to elect upon what counts of the indictment it will go to trial. The indictment charges in nine counts, that on three occasions Mr Weeks sent tickets by mail, and in six of the counts that he sent them by express. The meeting of these charges at the same time will embarass the defendant; and, together with that, a different punishment is, as I understand it, attached to sending the tickets by mail from that attached to sending them by express; and also sending the tickets by mail, if they were sent from a point in the state to a point within the state, would constitute a crime; but if they were sent by express, they would have to be sent beyond the limits of the

Discuss

- In *Weeks* v. *The United States*, the attorney for the Government argued that the law enforcement officers behaved logically during the investigation, based on the amount of incriminating evidence against Weeks. Do you think evidence seized without a warrant should be admissible in court if it's obvious that the accused is guilty?

- Prior to the *Weeks* decision, courts operated on the premise that the need for justice was of greater importance than the defendant's protection under the Fourth Amendment; and thus evidence obtained without a warrant was commonplace. The Court created the "exclusionary rule" in the *Weeks* decision. It forbids the use of illegally obtained evidence in federal court. Do you think this rule makes criminal prosecutions more difficult? Could it allow the guilty to go unpunished?

- Do you think the need for a search warrant to obtain evidence ever puts law enforcement at a disadvantage? If so, is it worth it?

Suspending the Right of Due Process: Japanese-American Relocation during WWII

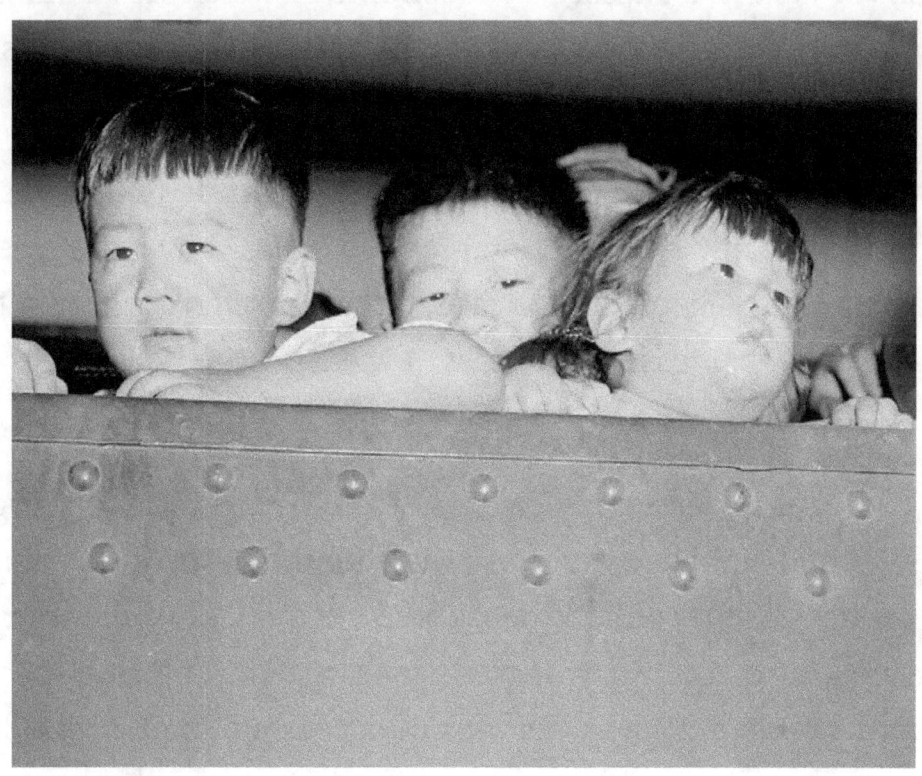

Following the Pearl Harbor bombing, in reaction to growing hysteria along the Pacific coast from Alaska to Southern California and in Hawaii, families of Japanese ancestry were sent to hastily built "relocation" camps further inland. These individuals were denied the constitutional right to due process through the courts because of perceived public danger.

The Fifth Amendment states:
> No person shall be held to answer for a capital, or otherwise infamous crime, unless on a presentment or indictment of a grand jury, except in cases arising in the land or naval forces, or in the militia, when in actual service in time of war or public danger...nor be deprived of life, liberty, or property, without due process of law...

Background

These persons of Japanese ancestry had committed no crimes. Almost two-thirds of them were American citizens. This included thousands of small children.

Because of the perception of "public danger," all Japanese within varied distances from the Pacific coast were targeted. Unless they were able to dispose of or make arrangements for care of their property within a few days, their homes, farms, businesses and most of their private belongings were lost forever.

First, they were sent to "assembly centers" – often racetracks or fairgrounds – where they waited and were tagged to indicate the location of a long-term "relocation center" that would be their home for the rest of the war.
Then they were sent by train or bus to their assigned Centers, which were often far from their homes, perhaps in different climates with harsh conditions. They were housed in army-style barracks, usually shared with several other families. Most lived in these conditions for nearly three years, sometimes more. Gradually some insulation was added to the barracks, and lightweight partitions were added to make them a little more comfortable and somewhat private.

During this period, three Japanese-American citizens were involved in legal actions in protest of this policy: Gordon Hirabayashi, Fred Korematsu, and Mitsuye Endo. Hirabayashi and Korematsu received negative judgments; but Mitsuye Endo, after a lengthy battle through lesser courts, was allowed to leave the Topaz, Utah, facility.

Justice Murphy of the Supreme Court expressed the following opinion:

> I join in the opinion of the Court, but I am of the view that detention in Relocation Centers of persons of Japanese ancestry regardless of loyalty is not only unauthorized by Congress or the Executive but is another

example of the unconstitutional resort to racism inherent in the entire evacuation program. As stated more fully in my dissenting opinion in *Fred Toyosaburo Korematsu* v. *United States*...racial discrimination of this nature bears no reasonable relation to military necessity and is utterly foreign to the ideals and traditions of the American people.

As World War II drew to a close, the relocation centers were slowly evacuated. Some persons of Japanese ancestry returned to their home towns and others moved elsewhere.

In 1988, President Reagan signed the Civil Liberties Act, awarding compensation and issuing a formal apology for the U.S. military action affecting over 100,000 Japanese-American civilians during World War II.

Think About

Do American citizens take their "inalienable rights" for granted?

Analyze the Document

Consider the following questions as you look at the sign on the next pages:

- What is the message in these instructions?

- Who is it directed to?

- Who are these instructions from?

- What is expected? When?

Document

The photograph on the following page shows one of the Exclusion Orders directing removal of persons of Japanese ancestry to be effected by the evacuation.

WESTERN DEFENSE COMMAND AND FOURTH ARMY
WARTIME CIVIL CONTROL ADMINISTRATION
Presidio of San Francisco, California
April 1, 1942

INSTRUCTIONS TO ALL PERSONS OF JAPANESE ANCESTRY

Living in the Following Area:

All that portion of the City and County of San Francisco, State of California, lying generally west of the north-south line established by Junipero Serra Boulevard, Worchester Avenue, and Nineteenth Avenue, and lying generally north of the east-west line established by California Street, to the intersection of Market Street, and thence on Market Street to San Francisco Bay.

All Japanese persons, both alien and non-alien, will be evacuated from the above designated area by 12:00 o'clock noon Tuesday, April 7, 1942.

No Japanese person will be permitted to enter or leave the above described area after 8:00 a. m., Thursday, April 2, 1942, without obtaining special permission from the Provost Marshal at the Civil Control Station located at:

1701 Van Ness Avenue
San Francisco, California

The Civil Control Station is equipped to assist the Japanese population affected by this evacuation in the following ways:

1. Give advice and instructions on the evacuation.
2. Provide services with respect to the management, leasing, sale, storage or other disposition of most kinds of property including: real estate, business and professional equipment, buildings, household goods, boats, automobiles, livestock, etc.
3. Provide temporary residence elsewhere for all Japanese in family groups.
4. Transport persons and a limited amount of clothing and equipment to their new residence, as specified below.

The Following Instructions Must Be Observed:

1. A responsible member of each family, preferably the head of the family, or the person in whose name most of the property is held, and each individual living alone, will report to the Civil Control Station to receive further instructions. This must be done between 8:00 a. m. and 5:00 p. m. Thursday, April 2, 1942, or between 8:00 a. m. and 5:00 p. m., Friday, April 3, 1942.

Discuss

- How do you think those who were sent to "relocation centers" settled back into their lives after they were allowed to leave?

- Could we ever be deprived of the rights guaranteed to us by the U.S. Constitution and its amendments without good reason? What might cause such a severe response?

- What far-reaching consequences might occur if we had even a temporary suspension of own rights?

Petitioning the Supreme Court for the Right to an Attorney

The Sixth Amendment's guarantee of the right to a lawyer has expanded significantly in recent history. The most important change occurred as a result of the *Gideon* v. *Wainwright* case in 1963.

The Sixth Amendment states:

> In all criminal prosecutions, the accused shall enjoy the right to a speedy and public trial, by an impartial jury of the State and district wherein the crime shall have been committed...and have the Assistance of Counsel for his defense.

Background

In June, 1961, Clarence Earl Gideon was arrested for breaking and entering in Florida. At the beginning of his trial in August, Gideon requested that the judge appoint a lawyer to defend him because he could not afford one. But the judge refused because Florida only provided free lawyers in capital cases. At that time, 37 of 50 States provided lawyers for poor defendants in all felony cases, and eight others usually provided lawyers in felony cases. Only five provided lawyers only in capital cases, and Florida was one of them. During his trial, Gideon unsuccessfully defended himself, and was convicted and sent to prison.

Although Gideon had only an eighth grade education, he filed a petition asking for a review of his case, based on the argument that he was being illegally held because he'd been denied a lawyer. The petition was rejected by the Florida courts. His subsequent petition to the Supreme Court was returned, along with a Supreme Court style manual. Writing on prison stationery and following the samples in the manual, Gideon resubmitted his request on January 5, 1962. Gideon also filed a request that the Supreme Court appoint a lawyer to present his case because he was "a pauper."

The Court appointed the respected Washington attorney Abe Fortas to represent Gideon. (Fortas was soon to become a Supreme Court Justice.) Fortas argued that a defendant could not get a fair trial in the United States without a lawyer and that conviction without a fair trial violated due process of law. In other words, those who could not afford a lawyer were being denied equal protection under the law.

Fortas's arguments convinced the Court. The unanimous Gideon decision required states to provide counsel for poor felony defendants. Gideon was retried in Florida, and his case was presented by a lawyer. He was found innocent, as he'd claimed he was all along.

Think About

Why would the right to a lawyer during trial be included in the Bill of Rights?

Analyze the Document

Consider the following questions as you look at the petition that Gideon submitted to the Supreme Court on the next pages:

- What does Gideon ask the Supreme Court to do?

- How does he describe the relationship between the Supreme Court and the Florida courts? Why does this matter?

- What parts of the Constitution does he mention? Why?

- A writ of certiorari is when the Supreme Court orders a lower court to send a case up to it for review. What reasons does Gideon give for the Supreme Court to hear his case?

- What does he say he was deprived of?

Document

The following pages are the petition that Gideon submitted to the Supreme Court in January, 1962, to overturn his conviction.

DIVISION OF CORRECTIONS
CORRESPONDENCE REGULATIONS

MAIL WILL NOT BE DELIVERED WHICH DOES NOT CONFORM WITH THESE RULES

No. 1 -- Only 2 letters each week, not to exceed 2 sheets letter-size 8 1/2 x 11" and written *on one side only*, and if ruled paper, do not write between lines. *Your complete name* must be signed at the close of your letter. *Clippings, stamps, letters* from other people, *stationery* or *cash* must not be enclosed in your letters.

No. 2 -- All *letters* must be addressed in the *complete prison name* of the inmate. *Cell number*, where applicable, and *prison number* must be placed in lower left corner of envelope, with your complete name and address in the upper left corner.

No. 3 -- *Do not send any packages without a Package Permit*. Unauthorized *packages* will be destroyed.

No. 4 -- *Letters* must be written in English only.

No. 5 -- *Books, magazines, pamphlets*, and *newspapers* of reputable character will be delivered *only if* mailed direct from the publisher.

No. 6 -- *Money* must be sent in the form of *Postal Money Orders* only, in the inmate's complete prison name and prison number.

INSTITUTION _____ CELL NUMBER _____

NAME _____ NUMBER _____

In The Supreme Court of The United States
            Washington D.C.

Clarence Earl Gideon,   )
        Petitioner   ) Petition for a Writ
    vs.   ) of Certiorari Directed
H.G. Cochran, Jr., as   ) to The Supreme Court
Director, Divisions   ) State of Florida.
of Corrections State   )
of Florida   )

No. 890 Misc.
OCT. TERM 1961
U.S. Supreme Court

To: The Honorable Earl Warren, Chief
    Justice of the United States

Comes now the petitioner, Clarence Earl Gideon, a citizen of The United States of America, in proper person, and appearing as his own counsel. Who petitions this Honorable Court for a Writ of Certiorari directed to The Supreme Court of The State of Florida. To review the order and judgement of the court below denying The petitioner a Writ of Habeus Corpus.

Petitioner submits That The Supreme Court of The United States has the authority and jurisdiction to review the final judgement of The Supreme Court of The State of Florida the highest court of The State under sec. 344(B) Title 28 U.S.C.A. and Because The "Due process clause" of the

DIVISION OF CORRECTIONS
CORRESPONDENCE REGULATIONS

MAIL WILL NOT BE DELIVERED WHICH DOES NOT CONFORM WITH THESE RULES

No. 1 -- Only 2 letters each week, not to exceed 2 sheets letter-size 8 1/2 x 11" and written *on one side only*, and if ruled paper, do not write between lines. *Your complete name* must be signed at the close of your letter. *Clippings, stamps, letters* from other people, *stationery* or *cash must not be enclosed* in your letters.

No. 2 -- All *letters* must be addressed in the *complete prison name* of the inmate. *Cell number*, where applicable, and *prison number* must be placed in lower left corner of envelope, with your complete name and address in the upper left corner.

No. 3 -- *Do not send any packages without a Package Permit.* Unauthorized *packages* will be destroyed.
No. 4 -- *Letters* must be written in English only.
No. 5 -- *Books, magazines, pamphlets,* and *newspapers* of reputable character will be delivered *only if* mailed direct from the publisher.
No. 6 -- *Money* must be sent in the form of *Postal Money Orders* only, in the inmate's complete prison name and prison number.

INSTITUTION _____ CELL NUMBER _____

NAME _____ NUMBER _____

fourteenth admendment of the constitution and the fifth and sixth articales of the Bill of rights has been violated. Furthermore, the decision of the court below denying the petitioner a Writ of Habeus Corpus is also inconsistent and adverse to its own previous decisions in perrelled cases.

Attached hereto, and made a part of this petition is a true copy of the petition for a Writ of Habeus Corpus as presented to the Florida Supreme Court. Petitioner asks this Honorable Court to cosider the same arguments and authorities cited in the petition for Writ of Habeus Corpus before the Florida Supreme Court, In consideration of this petition for a Writ of Certiorari.

The Supreme Court of Florida did not write any opinion. Order of that court denying petition for Writ of Habeus Corpus dated October 30, 1961, are attached hereto and made a part of this petition.

Petitioner contends that he has been deprived of due process of law Habeus Corpus petition alleging that the lower state court has decided a

DIVISION OF CORRECTIONS
CORRESPONDENCE REGULATIONS

MAIL WILL NOT BE DELIVERED WHICH DOES NOT CONFORM WITH THESE RULES

No. 1 -- Only 2 letters each week, not to exceed 2 sheets letter-size 8 1/2 x 11" and written *on one side only*, and if ruled paper, do not write between lines. *Your complete name* must be signed at the close of your letter. *Clippings, stamps, letters* from other people, *stationery* or *cash* must not be enclosed in your letters.

No. 2 -- All *letters* must be addressed in the *complete prison name* of the inmate. *Cell number*, where applicable, and *prison number* must be placed in lower left corner of envelope, with your complete name and address in the upper left corner.

No. 3 -- *Do not send any packages without a Package Permit.* Unauthorized *packages* will be destroyed.
No. 4 -- *Letters* must be written in English only.
No. 5 -- *Books, magazines, pamphlets,* and *newspapers* of reputable character will be delivered *only if* mailed direct from the publisher.
No. 6 -- *Money* must be sent in the form of *Postal Money Orders* only, In the inmate's complete prison name and prison number.

INSTITUTION _____ CELL NUMBER _____

NAME _____ NUMBER _____

federal question of substance, in a way not in accord with the applicable decisions of this Honorable court. When at the time of the petitioners trial. He ask the lower court for the aid of counsel. The court refused this aid Petitioner told the court that this court had made decision to the effect that all citizens tried for a felony crime should have aid of counsel. The lower court ignored this plea.

Petitioner alleges that prior to petitioners convictions and sentence for Breaking and Entering with the intent to commit petty larceny, he had requested aid of counsel, that, at the time of his conviction and sentence, petitioner was without aid of counsel. That the Court refused and did not appoint counsel, and that he was incapable adequately of making his own defense. In consequence of which he was made to stand trial. Made a Prima Facia showing of denial of due process of law. (U.S.C.A. Const Amend. 14) William V. Kaiser vs. State of Missouri 65 C.T. 363 Counsel must be assigned to the accused if he is unable to employ

DIVISION OF CORRECTIONS
CORRESPONDENCE REGULATIONS

MAIL WILL NOT BE DELIVERED WHICH DOES NOT CONFORM WITH THESE RULES

No. 1 -- Only 2 letters each week, not to exceed 2 sheets letter-size 8 1/2 x 11" and written *on one side only*, and if ruled paper, do not write between lines. *Your complete name* must be signed at the close of your letter. *Clippings, stamps, letters* from other people, *stationery* or *cash must not be enclosed* in your letters.

No. 2 -- All *letters* must be addressed in the *complete prison name* of the inmate. *Cell number*, where applicable, and *prison number* must be placed in lower left corner of envelope, with your complete name and address in the upper left corner.

No. 3 -- *Do not send any packages without a Package Permit.* Unauthorized *packages* will be destroyed.

No. 4 -- *Letters* must be written in English only.

No. 5 -- *Books, magazines, pamphlets,* and *newspapers* of reputable character will be delivered *only if* mailed direct from the publisher.

No. 6 -- *Money* must be sent in the form of *Postal Money Orders* only, in the inmate's complete prison name and prison number.

INSTITUTION _____ CELL NUMBER _____

NAME _____ NUMBER _____

one, and is incapable adequately of making his own defense
Tomkins vs State Missouri 65 ct 370

On the 3rd June 1961 A.D. your Petitioner was arrested for foresaid crime and convicted for same, Petitioner recieve Trial and sentence without aid of counsel, your petitioner was deprived "Due process of law".

Petitioner was deprived of due process of law in the court. Evidence in the lower court did not show that a crime of Breaking and Entering with the intent to commit Petty Larceny had been committed. Your petitioner was compelled to make his own defense, he was incapable adequately of making his own defense Petitioner did not plead nolo contender But that is what his trial amounted to.

DIVISION OF CORRECTIONS
CORRESPONDENCE REGULATIONS

MAIL WILL NOT BE DELIVERED WHICH DOES NOT CONFORM WITH THESE RULES

No. 1 -- Only 2 letters each week, not to exceed 2 sheets letter-size 8 1/2 x 11" and written *on one side only*, and if ruled paper, do not write between lines. *Your complete name* must be signed at the close of your letter. *Clippings, stamps, letters* from other people, *stationery* or *cash* must not be enclosed in your letters.

No. 2 -- All *letters* must be addressed in the *complete prison name* of the inmate. *Cell number*, where applicable, and *prison number* must be placed in lower left corner of envelope, with your complete name and address in the upper left corner.

No. 3 -- *Do not send any packages without a Package Permit.* Unauthorized *packages* will be destroyed.

No. 4 -- *Letters* must be written in English only.

No. 5 -- *Books, magazines, pamphlets,* and *newspapers* of reputable character will be delivered *only if* mailed direct from the publisher.

No. 6 -- *Money* must be sent in the form of *Postal Money Orders* only, in the inmate's complete prison name and prison number.

INSTITUTION _____ CELL NUMBER _____

NAME _____ NUMBER _____

Wherefore the premises considered it is respectfully contented that the decision of the court below was in error and the case should be review by this court, accordingly the writ prepared and, prayed for should be issue.

IT is respectfully submitted

Clarence Earl Gideon
Clarence Earl Gideon
P.O. Box 221
Raiford Florida

State of Florida)
County of Union) ss

Petitioner Clarence Earl Gideon, personally appearing before me and being duly sworn. Affirms, that the foregoing petition and the facts set forth in the petition are correct and true

Sworn and subcribed before me this 5th. day of Jan 1962

Lawrence Dwyer
Notary Public

Discuss

- Justice Hugo Black wrote the opinion for the Supreme Court requiring Florida to provide counsel for Clarence Earl Gideon. In the following paragraph from Justice Black's decision, why does he claim having an attorney is "fundamental"?

    > Reason and reflection require us to recognize that in our adversary system of criminal justice, any person hailed into court, who is too poor to hire a lawyer, cannot be assured a fair trial unless counsel is provided for him. This seems to be an obvious truth....That government hires lawyers to prosecute and defendants who have the money hire lawyers to defend are the strongest indications of the widespread belief that lawyers in criminal courts are necessities, not luxuries. The right of one charged with crime to counsel may not be deemed fundamental and essential to fair trials in some countries, but it is in ours.

- Do you think that defendants whose attorney's are hired by the state to defend them receive the same quality of representation as defendants who have the money to hire an attorney themselves? Do you think they should?

- The Supreme Court doesn't grant a writ of certiorari often, and "usually only if the case could have national significance, might harmonize conflicting decisions in the federal Circuit courts, and/or could have precedential value. In fact, the Court accepts 100-150 of the more than 7,000 cases that it is asked to review each year." (http://www.uscourts.gov) What about Gideon's case do you think the Supreme Court thought was worth hearing?

Is the Death Penalty a Cruel and Unusual Punishment?

America's Founders witnessed a time when branding, ear cropping, drawing and quartering, and other methods of torture were commonplace. In order to safeguard citizens from excessive punishment the Eighth Amendment ensures individuals protection from cruel and unusual punishment: "Excessive bail shall not be required, nor excessive fines imposed, nor cruel and unusual punishments inflicted."

Background

In 1900, eighteen people in Van Buren County, Arkansas, felt compelled to petition the government and express their disagreement with capital punishment. Both the group's freedom of expression and right to petition the government are protected by the First Amendment, but the issue they raised directly relates to the Eighth Amendment.

For the petitioners, capital punishment or the death penalty, was simply murder. They felt individuals should not be put to death, but could be rehabilitated after much introspection and reflection. The petitioners' goal was to have Congress abolish the death penalty and for America to take its place as a moral leader of the world.

Think About

- What is cruel and unusual punishment and who decides what is considered cruel and unusual?

- How can it be measured?

Analyze the Document

Consider the following questions as you look at the petition on the next pages:

- What do the petitioners define capital punishment to be?

- What do they hope will happen to capital punishment? What do they believe is an alternative?

- What do they believe to be "pure Justice" and how can it be obtained?

- What do they mean by "Humanitarianism"?

- What do you think their main influence is for writing this petition?

Document

The following page is a petition sent to Congress in 1900 to abolish the death penalty.

THE LIGHT OF TRUTH.

PETITION.

TO THE SENATE AND HOUSE OF REPRESENTATIVES OF THE UNITED STATES.

THE taking of life by the machinery of the law is none the less murder actually; hence, capital punishment MUST be abolished throughout America before better moral conditions will obtain.

Solitary confinement for life is recommended for offenses which today merit life-imprisonment or hanging. Face to face with his own real self, man reviews his life and sees the mistakes of the Past, and this introspection and retrospection will lead him to purge his spirit from all debasing, criminal intent, and he will have become changed for the better before passing into the other life. Let the product of his labor be sold, and the money thus derived be given to the support or assistance of the surviving members of the family he has disrupted. This is the only rational, merciful mode of reformation, and the only one which inures to the betterment of him who administers and him who receives, and is, we think, only pure Justice.

The eyes of the whole world are upon America, the friend to the oppressed of other countries. Let her luster be grandly increased by this step towards a higher civilization—"Humanitarianism." The coming centuries can record no greater deed than this: therefore be it

Resolved, That we, the undersigned voters of America, will and do hereby pray your honorable body to give the subject of this petition solemn consideration, and to immediately frame and enact such law as will accomplish what we have hereinbefore suggested and do hereby earnestly urge be done, abolishing **FOREVER** capital punishment throughout the United States of America:

NAME.	ADDRESS.			
J. Embra McMahel	Diamond	Van Buren Co., Ark.		
[illegible] Wheatley	[illegible]	"	"	"
J. W. Yarber	Diamond	"	"	"
Jas. [illegible]	Diamond			
Isaac Davis	Diamond	"		Ark.
[illegible] Emerson	[illegible]			
A. J. McMahel	Okay	"	"	"
M. I. Austin	"	"	"	"
P. J. [illegible]	Diamond	"	"	
[illegible]	Diamond			
S. M. C. Yarber	Diamond			Ark.
D. J. Yarber	Diamond			Ark.
W. E. Yarber	Diamond			Ark.
Joseph Roper	Okay			
Robert McMahel	Diamond	"		Ark.
E. M. McMahel	"	"		"
A. A. McMahel	"	"		"
L. M. Lawless	Okay	"	"	Ark.

Discuss

- What feelings are the petitioners hoping to evoke from the members of Congress by titling the petition "The Light of Truth"?

- What does cruel and unusual mean? How is the cruelty of a punishment measured? Who decides if a punishment is cruel and unusual?

- Read the following phrase from the Fifth Amendment: "No person shall be held to answer for a capital, or otherwise infamous crime,…nor be deprived of life, liberty, or property, without due process of law." How should the Fifth and Eight Amendments be balanced? Based on this, do you believe the Founders felt that capital punishment was an appropriate punishment as long as a person had received proper due process?

Document Citations

Cover

Photograph P80268_33; Participants and Flag at a Civil Rights Event at the Edmund Pettus Bridge in Selma, Alabama; 3/5/2000; Photographs Relating to the Clinton Administration, 1/20/1993 - 1/20/2001; Collection WJC-WHPO: Photographs of the White House Photograph Office (Clinton Administration); William J. Clinton Library, Little Rock, AR. [Online Version, https://www.docsteach.org/documents/document/civil-rights-event-selma]

Rights: Public Domain, Free of Known Copyright Restrictions

"Freedom of" or "Freedom From" Religion?

Photograph 306-PSD-68-4049c; Rising Earth Greets Apollo 8 Astronauts; 12/29/1968; Master File Photographs of U.S. and Foreign Personalities, World Events, and American Economic, Social, and Cultural Life, ca. 1953 - ca. 1994; Records of the U.S. Information Agency, Record Group 306; National Archives at College Park, College Park, MD. [Online Version, https://www.docsteach.org/documents/document/rising-earth-greets-apollo-8-astronauts]

Rights: Public Domain, Free of Known Copyright Restrictions

Memorandum Opinion; 12/1/1969; *Madalyn Murray O'Hair, et. al.* v. *Thomas O. Paine, et. al.* (A-69-CA-109); Civil Case Files, 1938 - 1996; Records of District Courts of the United States, Record Group 21; National Archives at Fort Worth, Fort Worth, TX. [Online Version, https://www.docsteach.org/documents/document/ohair-opinion]

Rights: Public Domain, Free of Known Copyright Restrictions

Freedom of Speech for the Masses

Opinion in *Masses Publishing Company v. T. G. Patten*; 7/24/1917 - 9/7/1917; E14-225; *Masses Publishing Company v. T. G. Patten, Postmaster of the City of New York*; Equity Case Files, 1868 - 1975; Records of District Courts of the United States, Record Group 21; National Archives at New York, New York, NY. [Online Version, https://www.docsteach.org/documents/document/masses-v-patten-opinion]

Rights: Public Domain, Free of Known Copyright Restrictions

Freedom to Cover the World Series

View of the Players' Locker Room and Cubicles; 1978; 77C6301; *Melissa Ludtke and Time, Incorporated v. Bowie Kuhn, Commissioner of Baseball, et al.*; (Civil Case Files, 1962 - 1979); Records of District Courts of the United States, Record Group 21; National Archives at New York, New York, NY. [Online Version, https://www.docsteach.org/documents/document/players-locker-room]

Rights: No Known Copyright

Complaint; 12/29/1977; 77C6301; *Melissa Ludtke and Time, Incorporated v. Bowie Kuhn, Commissioner of Baseball, et al.*; Civil Case Files , 1962 - 1979; Records of District Courts of the United States, Record Group 21; National Archives at New York, New York, NY. [Online Version, https://www.docsteach.org/documents/document/ludtke-complaint]

Rights: Public Domain, Free of Known Copyright Restrictions

Freedom of the Press Under Stress

The United States v. Ann Greenleaf; 2/9/1799; Criminal Case Files, 1790 - 1912; Records of District Courts of the United States, Record Group 21; National

Archives at New York, New York, NY. [Online Version, https://www.docsteach.org/documents/document/greenleaf-indictment]

Rights: Public Domain, Free of Known Copyright Restrictions

Permission to "Take it to the Streets"

Protestors on Michigan Avenue in Chicago; 8/28/1968; 69CR180; *United States v. Dellinger, et al.*; Criminal Case Files, 1873 - 1991; Records of District Courts of the United States, Record Group 21; National Archives at Chicago, Chicago, IL. [Online Version, https://www.docsteach.org/documents/document/protestors-on-michigan-avenue]

Rights: No Known Copyright

City of Chicago Department of Streets and Sanitation Application; 7/25/1968; 69CR180; *United States v. Dellinger, et al.*; Criminal Case Files, 1873 - 1991; Records of District Courts of the United States, Record Group 21; National Archives at Chicago, Chicago, IL. [Online Version, https://www.docsteach.org/documents/document/city-of-chicago-department-of-streets-and-sanitation-application]

Rights: Public Domain, Free of Known Copyright Restrictions

A Seditious Petition

Alien and Sedition Acts of 1798; 6/25/1798 - 7/14/1798; Enrolled Acts and Resolutions of Congress, 1789 - 2011; General Records of the United States Government, Record Group 11; National Archives Building, Washington, DC. [Online Version, https://www.docsteach.org/documents/document/alien-and-sedition-acts]

Rights: Public Domain, Free of Known Copyright Restrictions

The United States v. *Jedediah Peck*; 6/27/1799; Criminal Case Files, 1790 - 1912; Records of District Courts of the United States, Record Group 21; National Archives at New York, New York, NY. [Online Version, https://www.docsteach.org/documents/document/indictment-jedediah-peck]

Rights: Public Domain, Free of Known Copyright Restrictions

Examining the Second Amendment

Letter from J. M. Blough to the National Law Enforcement Commission Requesting Legislation to Restrict the Purchase of Firearms; 9/10/1929; B 1929 [3/5]; General Correspondence, 1930 - 1931; Records of the National Commission on Law Observance and Enforcement, Record Group 10; National Archives at College Park, College Park, MD. [Online Version, https://www.docsteach.org/documents/document/request-legislation-restrict-firearms]

Rights: Copyright Not Evaluated

Letter from Charles Koch Opposed to Gun Control Laws; 12/3/1975; Administrative Files of the Subcommittee on Crime of the Committee on the Judiciary during the 94th Congress; Committee Papers, 1813 - 2011; Records of the U.S. House of Representatives, Record Group 233; National Archives Building, Washington, DC. [Online Version, https://www.docsteach.org/documents/document/letter-opposing-gun-control]

Rights: No Known Copyright

Suspending the Right of Due Process: Japanese-American Relocation During WWII

Photograph 210-G-D79; Eden, Idaho. Gerald, 5, David, 6 and Chester Sakura, Jr., 1-1/2, brothers. These little evacuees...; 8/17/1942; Central Photographic

File of the War Relocation Authority, 1942 - 1945; Records of the War Relocation Authority, Record Group 210; National Archives at College Park, College Park, MD. [Online Version, https://www.docsteach.org/documents/document/little-evacuees-minidoka]

Rights: Public Domain, Free of Known Copyright Restrictions

Photograph 210-G-A39; San Francisco, California. Exclusion Order posted at First and Front Streets; 4/11/1942; Central Photographic File of the War Relocation Authority, 1942 - 1945; Records of the War Relocation Authority, Record Group 210; National Archives at College Park, College Park, MD. [Online Version, https://www.docsteach.org/documents/document/exclusion-order]

Rights: Public Domain, Free of Known Copyright Restrictions

Search Warrants and the Fourth Amendment

Defendant's Bill of Exceptions; 11/6/1912; *The United States* v. *Fremont Weeks*; Criminal Case Files, 1879 - 1987; Records of District Courts of the United States, Record Group 21; National Archives at Kansas City, Kansas City, MO. [Online Version, https://www.docsteach.org/documents/document/defendants-bill-of-exceptions]

Rights: Public Domain, Free of Known Copyright Restrictions

Petitioning the Supreme Court for the Right to an Attorney

Petition for a Writ of Certiorari from Clarence Gideon to the Supreme Court of the United States; 1962; Appellate Jurisdiction Case File *Gideon* v. *Wainright*; Appellate Jurisdiction Case Files, 1792 - 2010; Records of the Supreme Court of the United States, Record Group 267; National Archives Building,

Washington, DC. [Online Version, https://www.docsteach.org/documents/document/gideon-petition-writ-certiorari]

Rights: Public Domain, Free of Known Copyright Restrictions

Is the Death Penalty Cruel and Unusual Punishment?

Bill of Rights; 9/25/1789; Enrolled Acts and Resolutions of Congress, 1789 - 2011; General Records of the United States Government, Record Group 11; National Archives Building, Washington, DC. [Online Version, https://www.docsteach.org/documents/document/bill-of-rights]

Rights: Public Domain, Free of Known Copyright Restrictions

Petition to Abolish the Death Penalty; 1900; Petitions and Memorials, Resolutions of State Legislatures, and Related Documents Which Were Referred to the Committee on the Judiciary during the 56th Congress; Petitions and Memorials, 1813 - 1968; Records of the U.S. House of Representatives, Record Group 233; National Archives Building, Washington, DC. [Online Version, https://www.docsteach.org/documents/document/petition-to-abolish-the-death-penalty]

Rights: Public Domain, Free of Known Copyright Restrictions

Rights and Reuse

To the extent possible under law, the National Archives has dedicated *Putting the Bill of Rights to the Test* to the public domain by waiving all rights to the work worldwide under copyright law, including all related and neighboring rights, to the extent allowed by law.

You can copy, modify, distribute, and perform the work, even for commercial purposes, all without asking permission.

If you use documents or images from this book, we ask that you include the citation provided or credit the National Archives as the source.